STEP-BY-STEP

Ami Pro 3.0
for
Windows

Dedication

To Stevie, Kim and Clare

Ami Pro 3.0
for
Windows

Moira Stephen

NEW·TECH

Newtech
An Imprint of Butterworth-Heinemann Ltd
Linacre House, Jordan Hill, Oxford OX2 8DP

Ɋ   A member of the Reed Elsevier group

OXFORD   LONDON   BOSTON
MUNICH   NEW DELHI   SINGAPORE   SYDNEY
TOKYO   TORONTO   WELLINGTON

First published 1993
© Moira Stephen 1993

NOTICE
The author and the publisher have used their best efforts to prepare this
book, including the computer examples contained in it. The computer
examples have all been tested. The author and the publisher make no
warranty, implicit or explicit, about the documentation. The author and
the publisher will not be liable under any circumstances for any direct
or indirect damages arising from any use, direct or indirect, of the
documentation or computer examples contained in this book.

TRADEMARKS/REGISTERED TRADEMARKS
Computer hardware and software brand names mentioned in this book
are protected by their respective trademarks and are acknowledged.

British Library Cataloguing in Publication Data
A catalogue record for this book is available from the British Library.

ISBN 0 7506 1698 9

Typeset by P.K.McBride, Southampton
Printed and bound in Great Britain

Moira Stephen is a college lecturer and consultant/ trainer, specialising in PC applications. She has also worked in sales and customer support roles for a number of computer companies, including ICL.

Contents

-1- Ami Pro 3.0 & Windows

-2- Basic Techniques

-3- Proofing Tools

-4- Beyond the Basics

Contents

Preface

In the late 70s, word processing was the domain of dedicated word processing machines. With the launch of the IBM PC and hordes of IBM compatibles in the early 80s, came a range of DOS based word processing packages from many suppliers. The latest phase in the evolution of word processing has come about due to the introduction and widespread adoption of the Windows environment in the 90s.

The later versions of Windows have allowed application software suppliers to exploit Windows' potential. Ami Pro version 3 is the current Lotus (one of the worlds' major PC software package suppliers) contender in the Windows based word processing package stakes.

This book takes you from the installation of the package, through the basic functions of creating, editing, printing and formatting, on to useful tools like sorting, merge and spell check and finally on to some of the more specialised features like tables, charts, equations, indexes and table of contents.

The functions are presented in straightforward, bite sized chunks that you can absorb readily, either at the machine, or as a "read" when the mood takes you.

The writer has found Ami Pro to be an enjoyable package to use and consequently the emphasis of the book is on the rapid development of Ami Pro skills, in a down to earth, non "heavy" approach. Practical examples are included in most chapters to reinforce the learning process.

This book should appeal to anyone who intends to get the most from Ami Pro in the shortest possible time.

Moira Stephen
Edinburgh, 1993

- 1 -
Ami Pro 3.0
&
Windows

The Windows environment isn't discussed fully in this book. It's anticipated that you'll have a basic knowledge of the environment. If you haven't used Windows before, I suggest that you browse through the on-line Windows tutorial (found in the Help menu in Program Manager) or read through Windows Fundamentals in the User's Guide and Reference.

I'll give you a whirlwind tour of some of the basics to give you an idea of what assumptions I'm making about your expertise in this area! Before going into Ami Pro, make sure you can answer YES to the following questions.

■ Can you identify the **Title Bar; Menu Bar; Minimise, Maximise and Restore buttons; Control Box**?

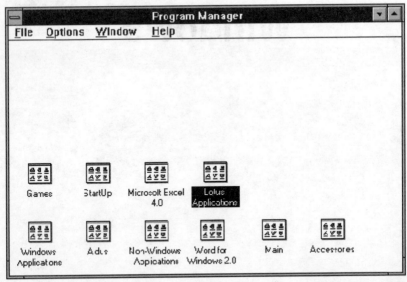

■ Do you know what a **Window Border, Group Icon** and **Application Icon** are?

■ Do you know the difference between an **Active** and **Inactive** Window?

Can you:-
Resize and **reposition** windows?
Access **Menus** and choose **Options** from them?
Use **Scroll bars** and **Boxes**?

When working in a Windows environment you often come across dialogue boxes like the one below.

You can specify whatever options you require through dialogue boxes. Items grouped together with checkboxes beside them (the small squares) can have as many or as few of the listed items selected as required. When selected an X appears in the checkbox. You select and de-select an item by clicking in the box.

Other grouped items have radio buttons beside them (the circles). You can only select ONE item from a list in this kind of group.

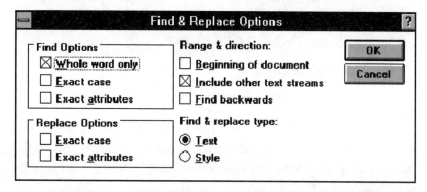

Some boxes, like the next one, have fields with an arrow pointing down at the right hand side of it - like the **Drives:** and **Files:** fields. Clicking on this arrow drops down a list of alternatives you can choose from.

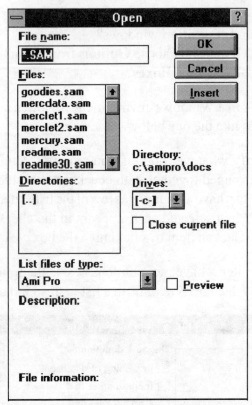

Throughout the book, Windows actions that are essential to make a function work will be described in detail at the appropriate time. However, as the use of Windows isn't covered in detail you might want to keep your Windows documentation handy!

To get the best from Ami Pro (and all other Windows packages), it's recommended you use a Mouse. ALL instructions in this book assume you're a Mouse-user and that you're familiar with clicking, double-clicking and click and drag techniques. If you haven't a mouse you'll find instructions on working in a Windows environment without a mouse in your Windows documentation, and instructions on getting about in Ami Pro in your Ami Pro documentation and on-line Help.

System Requirements for Ami Pro 3.0 are:-

SYSTEM REQUIREMENTS

Hardware	a 286, 386 or 486 based computer (certified for use with Microsoft Windows ver 3.x)
	an EGA, VGA, super VGA, or Hercules graphics card (compatible with Microsoft Windows ver 3.x)
	a Microsoft compatible mouse
	One of the following drive sizes:- 1.2Mb 5.25" disk drive or 1.44 Mb 3.5" disk drive or 720k 3.5" disk drive
System Software	Microsoft Windows ver 3.x or higher and DOS Ver 3.1 or higher (must be installed before you can set up Ami Pro)
Memory	Minimum of 2Mb RAM NB Ami Pro will not run in Windows Real mode
Disk Space	For a complete installation you'll need 12Mb For the minimum installation you'll need 5Mb

BEFORE YOU START

■ You must install Ami Pro from Program Manager in Windows.

■ Ami Pro files are transferred to your hard disk. If you log in as the network supervisor Ami Pro files are transferred to your network server.

■ Should you want stand-alone, network or NewWave installation information, it's all available on-line during the installation process. Choose **Help** (or press **F1**) from the dialogue boxes to get information. To print the details out choose **File,Print Topic** when the information is displayed in the Help window.

■ You can read or print all the on-line information before you install Ami Pro. To do this, start the installation process, then choose the **Help** button the first time it appears. Read or print the information on the various topics and then exit the Help Window.

■ You can then proceed with the installation or exit the install program by choosing the **Exit Install** button.

TO INSTALL AMI PRO

It's anticipated that you'll install Ami Pro from drive A - if you're not doing this, substitute the appropriate drive legend in the instructions below.

1 If Windows isn't running, go into Windows and open Program Manager. If you're working in Windows go back to the Program Manager Window.

2 Insert the Install Disk 1 in drive A

3 Choose **Run** from the **File** Menu

4 Type **A:INSTALL** and click **OK**

5 Specify your options in the dialogue boxes - if you're not sure what options you want click the **Help** button in the **Install Choices** dialogue box.

Your options are:-
- A stand-alone computer or a network server
- A Complete, Laptop, Custom or Options installation
- Whether you want to install Ami Pro for Windows or for NewWave
- The Drive and Directory for the Ami Pro program

UPGRADING FROM AN EARLIER RELEASE

NOTE:

You should install over the earlier release if you have one on your computer. You don't need to delete any files (Ami Pro won't automatically delete any during installation either). You must have Read/Write access to the Ami Pro directory and subdirectories on your disk.

Once Ami Pro 3.0 is installed you won't be able to run the earlier release.

Choose **Complete** or **Custom Ami Pro Install** from the **Choices** dialogue box and specify the same drive and directory as the earlier version.

DIRECTORIES FOR STYLE SHEETS, DOCUMENTS AND MACROS

During Install you'll be prompted for details of where you want to install style sheets, documents and macros.

Ami Pro 3.0 style sheets begin with **MERC*** or an underscore. If you've got style sheets with similar file names, you should specify a different directory for the version 3.0 style sheets. If you haven't, you can install into the existing directory.

During installation the following document files are installed into the DOCS directory:- README30.SAM, GOODIES.SAM, DEMO.SAM and a number of MERC*.* files. If you've created files with similar names, specify another directory for the Release 3.0 documents.

If you've modified macros provided with Ami Pro and saved them to the original files, specify another directory for the Release 3.0 macros, otherwise install into the existing one.

INSTALLING ON A NETWORK

Full details about installing on a Network can be found in READNET.TXT on install Disk 1 and the Installation Helps.

1   Log in as the network supervisor

2   Choose **Install Ami Pro as server**

3   Specify the network drive and directory you want Ami Pro installed in

4   You must specify a NODE directory (then the install program can install node-related files on the server).

5   Specify the number of Ami Pro licenses.

Once the installation is complete, use the NODE.EXE file to automate the process of setting up user nodes. (Run NODE.EXE from each workstation.)

STARTING AMI PRO

The method you use to start Ami Pro depends on whether Windows is already running or not. You can start Ami Pro from Windows Program Manager, or from the DOS prompt.

IF WINDOWS IS RUNNING

1   Display the **Program Manager** Window

2   Open the **Group** Window that contains the Ami Pro Icon

3   **Double Click** on the **Ami Pro** Icon

To start Ami Pro and open a Document

1   Open the Windows **File Manager**

2   Open the **Directory** window that contains the required document

3   **Double click** the **name of the document** you want to display

IF WINDOWS IS NOT RUNNING

1   Display a DOS prompt (eg **C:**) for the drive that contains Windows

2   Type **WIN AMIPRO** (if you didn't include the drive and directory that contain Ami Pro in the DOS path statement, you'll have to specify the complete path, eg:

    WIN C:\AMIPRO\AMIPRO

3   Press **Enter**

To start Ami Pro and Open a Document

Type the name of the document you want to open after starting Windows and Ami Pro.

1 Display a DOS prompt (eg **C:**) for the drive that contains Windows

2 Type **WIN AMIPRO FILENAME.SAM**

3 Press **Enter**

To start Ami Pro and Print a Document

Type **/P** followed by the name of the document you want to print after starting Windows and Ami Pro eg

1 Display a DOS prompt (eg **C:**) for the drive that contains Windows

2 Type **WIN AMIPRO /P FILENAME.SAM**

3 Press **Enter**

Now that you're in, take a good look at the Ami Pro Window.

THE AMI PRO WINDOW

Title Bar

This is along the top of the Window. It displays the name of the application and the document name, provided your document window is maximised. When you choose a **Menu** or **Menu Item** the Title Bar displays a one-line help message for your selection.

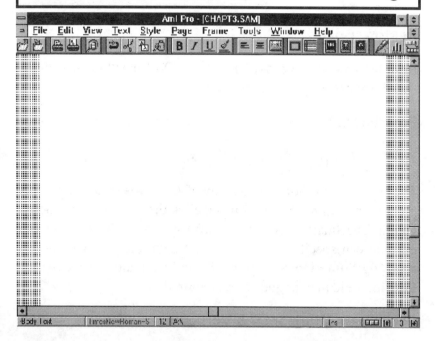

Control Menu Boxes (Application and Document)

These are displayed at the left of the Title Bar and Menu Bar. They display a menu that lets you restore, move, size, minimise, maximise, close the active window, switch between windows, or open the control panel window.

Menu Bar

This is below the Title Bar and it lists the main menus in Ami Pro.

Minimise Box

Reduces your Ami Pro window to an Icon at the bottom of the screen.

Maximise Box

Maximises your Ami Pro window to fill the screen.

Restore Boxes

Restores your Ami Pro Application or Document window to the size it was before you Maximised it.

SmartIcons

You MUST have a Mouse to use these.

These allow you shortcuts to many of Ami Pros features. Simply point to the desired SmartIcon and click the primary (left) mouse button. The SmartIcons are normally displayed under the Menu Bar but you can specify where you want them on your window by choosing **SmartIcons** from the **Tools** Menu and completing the **Position** field in dialogue box as required.

Scroll Bars (Horizontal & Vertical)

These are used to control the position of the document displayed on the screen.

Scroll Boxes (Horizontal & Vertical)

These indicate where the screen display is located compared to the full width of the document and where the **insertion point** is located in the document compared to the whole document.

Status Bar

The Status Bar displays information about the current document. Some buttons and icons in the Status Bar are *toggles* - they switch between modes or change the type of information displayed. The information displayed varies, depending on the function you're using.

Document Area

The "page" you will type onto is in the main area of the screen. The top, bottom, left and right margin areas of the page are shown in colour (unless you've modified this by choosing **View Preferences...** from the **View** menu, and de-selected the **Margins in Colour** checkbox).

The INSERTION point

This is the vertical black line in the first character position on the page. The insertion point shows you where your text will appear when you key data in through the keyboard.

EXITING AMI PRO

To Exit Ami Pro do any one of the following:-

■ **Double Click** the **Control Menu Box** (Mouse users)

■ Choose **Exit** from the **File** Menu

■ Press **ALT-F4**

If you've made changes to the current document, Ami Pro will present a dialogue box reminding you to save your document if you want to. Choose **Yes**, **No** or **Cancel** to remove the dialogue box and continue.

Before getting started with Ami Pro it is a good idea to familiarise yourself with some basic concepts and terms. Even if you're already familiar with word processing packages, a quick glance through this section will give you the answers to some of the questions that you'll probably ask in the early stages of using the package.

WYSIWYG

Ami Pro is a WYSIWYG word processor - What You See Is What You Get. This means that your document appears on the screen as it will print (this is not the case with all word processing packages). The only disadvantage you'll notice is that your screen will flicker a bit at times as Ami Pro re-writes it to reflect your input or edits. Don't worry about it - it's a small price to pay!

As far as using menus, menu commands, dialogue boxes, command buttons, option buttons, list boxes, check boxes and a mouse are concerned the package adheres to Microsoft Windows conventions. (If you're new to the Windows environment refer to the Microsoft Windows User's Guide On-line or Windows Help for assistance with the basics).

POINTER SHAPES

If you're using a Mouse one of the first things you'll notice is that the Pointer takes on different shapes depending on where it is and what you're doing.

The ones you'll see from day one are:-

I   The I-Beam

This is the shape the pointer assumes when in a TEXT area. If you click the left mouse button when you see an I-beam the insertion point moves to the position the I-beam was in.

ñ̃ Arrow

The pointer takes on an arrow shape when over Menus, Scroll Bars, the Status Bar, the Styles Box, Frames and SmartIcons.

6 Hourglass

The "wait" signal. When you see this you must wait for Ami Pro to perform a function.

ó Double Arrow

The pointer takes on this shape when you're over the border of a window when you size the window.

Other Pointer Shapes you'll encounter are:-

Hand

The mouse pointer takes on this shape inside a picture frame when you move the picture within the frame. It takes on a similar shape in the Help window when you access a cross-reference.

? Question Mark

When you press **Shift-F1** to use point-and-shoot help this is the shape the pointer assumes.

⊕ Small four-headed arrow

The mouse pointer takes on this shape over a table gridline when you size table cells

O Square Frame

When you create a frame manually this is the shape the mouse pointer takes.

ICONS & BUTTONS

As you work with Ami Pro you'll discover that there's more than one way to do most things. Everything you'll ever want to do can be done through the menus - but for many functions you'll find that there's a shortcut. An easy shortcut option for mouse users is through the icons and buttons on the screen.

SmartIcons

When you go into Ami Pro the SmartIcons are along the top of the window, below the menu bar. These SmartIcons can be used to automate many functions, commands and macros. To use a SmartIcon, point to it and click the left mouse button.

From left to right, the SmartIcons serve to:-

    Open an existing file
    Save the current file
    Print
    Print envelope
    Toggle Full Page view and Layout view
    Undo last command or action
    Cut to clipboard
    Copy to clipboard
    Paste from clipboard
    Bold text
    Italicise text
    Underline text
    Toggle fast format
    Left Align selected text
    Centre selected text

Toggle ruler display
Add a Frame
Create a Table
Spell check document
Thesaurus
Grammar Checker
Draw
Chart
Change set of SmartIcons displayed.

You can specify the location of the SmartIcons (Floating, Top, Bottom, Right or Left) by choosing **SmartIcons** from the **Tools** menu. Complete the **Position** field in the dialogue box as required.

Status Bar

The **Status Bar** is displayed along the bottom of the window. It displays information about the current document and provides icons and buttons for Ami Pro functions and commands. Some icons and buttons are "toggles" that either switch between modes or change the type of information displayed. To use the **Status Bar**, point at the icon or button required and click the left mouse button.

From left to right, the information on the Status Bar is:-

Style Status

This displays the name of the paragraph style for the current paragraph (ie the one the insertion point is in). When you click on the **Style Status** button you are presented with a list of the available paragraph styles. If you choose a paragraph style from the list Ami Pro assigns that style to the current paragraph.

Face

This displays the typeface for the text in which the insertion point is located. If you click on this button you're presented with a list of available typefaces. Choose a type face and Ami Pro assigns that face to the text selected.

(The type face displayed can be the one specified in the paragraph style you are using or a type face you've applied using the **Text** menu or **Status Bar**).

Point Size

This displays the point size of the text in which the insertion point is located. Clicking on this button displays a list of the available sizes. Choose a size and Ami Pro assigns it to the selected text.

(The point size can be the size specified by the paragraph style you're using or it can be one you've applied using the **Text** menu or **Status Bar**).

Document Path

This button displays the path name for the current document, the current date and time, or the current line, column and position within the document. It is a toggle - clicking on the button switches between path name, current date and time, and the line, column and position of the insertion point.

(The position of the insertion point reflects the unit of measurement specified in the current ruler).

Insert

This is another toggle button. It displays "**Ins**" if you're in Insert mode "**Type**" if you're in Typeover mode and "**Rev**" if you're in

Revision Marking mode. Clicking on the button switches you from one mode to another.

Caps Lock

If you've got your Caps Lock on, this button displays "**Caps**". If your Caps Lock is not on, then the button is blank.

Change or Show/Hide SmartIcons

Click the **SmartIcon** button to display a list of sets available. Choose the desired set option from the list by clicking on it.

Page Arrows

The UP and DOWN arrows are displayed regardless of where the insertion point is located in the document.

If you're in **Layout** Mode, clicking on an arrow moves the insertion point up or down to the next page. If you're in **Draft** Mode, clicking on an arrow moves the insertion point to the next or previous screen.

Page Status

This displays the current page number. The page number is only displayed in Layout Mode. Clicking on the **Page Status** icon displays the **GO TO** dialogue box.

You can save yourself a considerable amount of time by using the icons and buttons provided. We'll look at some more shortcuts later - meantime, get used to these ones as you work.

Don't panic, you don't have to remember them all at once - you can practice as you go!

One of your best friends when you're new to a package is the On-Line Help facility. Ami Pro provides on-line help for EVERY function.

There are 3 ways to get help - try them all and see how you get on. They are:-

■ Context Sensitive Help

■ Point and Shoot Help

■ Indexed Help

Ami Pro also provides a one line help message in the Title Bar when you select a Menu or choose a Menu Item.

CONTEXT SENSITIVE HELP

1 Choose a Menu

2 Choose a Menu Command

3 When a dialogue box displays press **F1** or click the **?** in the top right hand corner of the dialogue box

Ami Pro displays the appropriate Help Topic. When you close the Help screen you are returned to the dialogue box that you were in when you requested Help.

POINT & SHOOT HELP

1 Press **Shift-F1**

2 Choose a Menu

3 Choose a Menu Command

Ami Pro displays the appropriate Help topic

Either or these methods is recommended, especially when you're new to the package. They take you directly to the Help you need.

You might find that, at first, you get a bit lost going in through the Index (described next) because you don't know what topics have been called. Once you start to get used to the terminology, try using the index to look up whatever interests (or puzzles) you!

INDEXED HELP

Open the **Help** Menu to display the following options:-

Contents
Using Help
Keyboard
How Do I?
For Upgraders
Quickstart Tutorial ...
Macro Doc ...
Enhancement Products ...
About Ami Pro

Contents

Lists all categories of Help Topics. You can get to any part of the Help system from the Help Contents list.

Using Help

Provides information on using Help.

Keyboard

Lists the keyboard shortcuts for functions and commands.

How Do I?

Lists common functions and provides information on each one.

For Upgraders

Highlights improvements and major differences between the current release and previous versions

Quickstart Tutorial

Takes you through some short (5 mins on average) lessons on the package.

Macro Doc

If you've installed the on-line Macro documentation you can access it through Help

Enhancement Products

Gives details of other Windows applications and services to complement Ami Pro

About Ami Pro

Information about Ami Pro eg copyright, available memory.

Using Indexed Help

Select the Topic you want Help on - point and click using the Mouse or Cursor Up or Down until the option you want is highlighted, then press **Enter.**

eg. If you select **Contents** you get

> Basics
> How Do I?
> Keyboard
> Macros

Menus
Messages
Mouse
NewWave
Parts of the Ami Pro Window
SmartIcons

If you press **F1** on the Keyboard while in your document you go straight through to the Ami Pro Help Contents list as above.

You can work your way through Help in this way until you have the answer to your problem.

Cross-References

At the end of a Help item, you may find a Cross-Reference. To access this simply choose the Cross Reference as you would any Help item (point and click).

To get out of Help

Double click the **Control Menu Box** or choose **File/Exit.**

Help Buttons

While in Help you can use the **Help Buttons** to display the related Help topics. To use the Buttons simply choose the one you want - point and click with the left mouse button or hold down the **CTRL** key while pressing the underlined letter in the button.

Contents

Displays a list of Help Topics

Search

Lists all the Help keywords for Ami Pro so you can search for help on a particular topic.

Back

Displays the last topic you viewed

History

Lists the help screens you've accessed, from first to most recent, during the current dip into Help.

Help Menus

While in Help the **Help Menu Bar** displays the Help Menus available.

File

Opens Help files, prints Help topics, sets printer options and closes Help

Edit

Copies Help text to the Clipboard and adds annotation to Help text.

Bookmark

Lets you define bookmarks for Help topics.

Help

Tells you how to use Help, lets you specify whether or not the Help window appears on top of all other windows and gives you information about help.

The on-line Help is a very useful tool - it's often quicker than resorting to the manual or other published material.(!)

It's useful when you get stuck, but it's also a good idea to take a look through any topics that interest you when you get time. You'll be amazed at the tips and tricks that you find!!

-2-
Basic
Techniques

As soon as you've started Ami Pro, you can start typing up your document. A new document is automatically opened for you. The left and right margins are set to 1", as are the top and bottom ones. If this is okay for your document then you can just get started!

WORD-WRAP

Try typing up the passage below to get the feel of the keyboard and see how some of the basics work. DON'T press the **Enter** key at the end of your typing line - just keep going. The text will be wrapped onto the next line for you.

The only time that you need to press the **Enter** key is at the end of short lines - like salutations and address lines - or between paragraphs, where you press the **Enter** key TWICE so you leave a clear line space.

Don't worry about any typing errors you make - we'll fix them later!

PLACES TO VISIT IN THE SCOTTISH BORDERS

There are many interesting places to visit in the Scottish Borders. The area itself is very picturesque at any time of year with its hills, rivers, woods and historic towns.

There are many interesting towns and villages to visit - some are quite industrial while others are very rural. The people in any of them will extend a warm welcome to visitors.

Places of particular interest include the Abbeys at Jedburgh, Kelso, Melrose, and Dryburgh, Scott's View the Lammermuir hills themselves.

MOVING THE INSERTION POINT

Now that you're finished, check through to see if you've any mistakes.

You can move the insertion point to any place in your document by pointing and clicking with the left mouse button.

If the text you want to see is not within the window use the vertical or horizontal scroll bars to move larger distances.

You MUST remember to click the left mouse button to actually move the insertion point to where you want it to go!!

You can also move over the text by using the cursor (arrow) keys.

DELETE CHARACTERS

Position the insertion point either to the right or left of the character to be deleted.

Press the **Delete** key to delete the character to the right of the insertion point

OR

Press the **Backspace** key (above **Enter**) to delete the character to the left of the insertion point.

INSERT CHARACTERS

Position the insertion point where you wish to add a character - or any number of characters - you may have a few paragraphs to type in.

Type the new text required - the existing text will move to the right to make room for whatever you type in.

INSERT VS TYPEOVER MODE

The DEFAULT typing mode in Ami Pro is **INSERT** (Notice the **INS** button on the status bar at the bottom that indicates Insert Mode).

The alternative to Insert Mode is **TYPEOVER** Mode. When in Typeover mode, existing text is replaced by any new text you key in to it - the new text types over the old. (The button on the Status bar says **TYPE** when you're in Typeover Mode).

The toggle (the way you move between Insert and Typeover mode) is the **Insert** key on your keyboard. You can also use the **Ins** button on the Status bar to take you into Typeover - it takes you into Revision Marking Mode too (you just click it to circle through the 3 options).

Try experimenting with the two methods to see how they work.

NOTE

■ The **Delete** key and **Insert** key are next to each other on most keyboards, so it's quite easy to go into Typeover mode by mistake when you go to press the **Delete** key.

Try making the changes suggested on the next page.

PLACES TO VISIT IN THE SCOTTISH BORDERS
very
There are many/ interesting places to visit in the ~~Scottish~~
Borders. The area ~~itself~~ is very picturesque at any time of
year with its hills, rivers, woods and historic towns.

There are many interesting towns and villages to visit ⊙
Some are quite industrial while others are very rural. The
people in any of them will extend a warm welcome to
visitors.

Places of particular interest include the Abbeys at Jedburgh,
Kelso, Melrose, and Dryburgh, Scott's View ⊙ the
Lammermuir ~~hills themselves.~~ *and Cheviot Hills*.

SAVE

To save your document to disk do ONE of the following:-

■ Click the **Save** SmartIcon (2nd from the left)

■ Select **Save** from the **File** menu

■ Select **Save As** from the **File** menu

Any of the above takes you to the **SAVE AS** dialogue box.

Complete the dialogue box as required, ie:

1 Change drive if necessary - click the down arrow to the right of
the **Drives** field and select the required drive from the list given.

2   Select the required directory if necessary from the **Directories** box.

3   Type in the filename of your choice in the **Filename** box.

4   Click the **OK** button.

The first time you save a new document it doesn't matter which of the 3 methods you use, they all take you through to the **Save As** dialogue box so you can specify a drive, directory and name for your file. Once a file has been saved, and you want to save it again (after editing perhaps) they work a bit differently.

If you use the **SmartIcon** or **File/Save** to re-save a file you will OVERWRITE the file on disk with the one in memory (on the screen). The same drive, directory and filename will be assumed. Most of the time this is what you'll want to do as you replace an old version of a file with a new one.

File/Save As will take you into the **Save As** dialogue box so you can change the drive, directory or file name. This lets you keep the existing version of a file and also save the edited version under a different name and/or in a different location.

So, if you want to replace the old version of the file you're working on with the new edited version use the **SmartIcon** or **File/Save**.

If you want to keep the original file AND save the new, edited version, use **File/Save As** and change the drive, directory and/or name as required.

PRINT

1 Click the **Print** SmartIcon (3rd from left)

OR

Select **Print** from the **File** menu

2 Complete the dialogue box as required - with the short practice passage above the default suggestions will do.

3 Click the **OK** button

CLOSE

Once your file is saved and printed, you might want to move on and do another document.

CLOSE the one you're in by:

- Double clicking the **Control Box** at the left end of the Menu Bar
  OR
- Selecting **Close** from the **File** menu

CREATING A NEW FILE

To continue working, you'll want to start a new Document.

1 Choose **New** from the **File** Menu. The **New File** dialogue box appears.

2 You can select from various style sheets, but at this stage choose the default by clicking the **OK** button.

A lot of the time spent using a word processing package goes in creating, saving and printing new documents as you did in the previous section.

You'll also spend a lot of time EDITING documents that already exist - you'll need to open a document that you created earlier, make changes to it and save and print the modified version.

To enhance the appearance of your text you will want to use some Text formatting options.

Let's look at some ways we can enhance the appearance of Text. The possibilities fall into 6 main categories:-

- Formatting of the characters themselves using underline, bold, italics etc
- Alignment of the typing line (justification)
- Line spacing
- Font style and size
- Indentation of paragraphs from the left and right margins
- Fast Formatting

We'll look at the first 3 in this section

Create a new document to experiment with the features. If you're already in a document Save it and Close it.

To create a new document choose **New** from the **File** menu. Accept **_DEFAULT.STY** as the style sheet on which to base the document and click **OK**.

BOLD, UNDERLINE, ITALICS & OTHER EFFECTS

Text can be formatted very easily. The basic technique is the same for most character formatting instructions.

ENHANCING NEW TEXT

If you are typing new text in, and you know you want it bold, underlined or in italics you follow the sequence below:-

1   Switch the code on by clicking the **SmartIcon** or by choosing the option from the **Text** Menu

2   Type the text

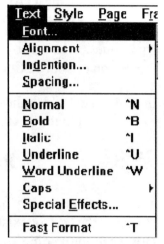

3   Switch the code off again by clicking the **SmartIcon** or by choosing the option from the **Text** Menu. (An option selected from the Menu has a tick beside it. Choosing the option again switches it off).

(If you have switched on a few options, they can all be switched off at once by choosing **Normal** from the **Text** Menu)

Try typing your name and todays date in your new document. Make your name bold and put the date into italics.

Position the insertion point where you want to insert your name

1   Switch on the BOLD by clicking the **B** SmartIcon or by choosing **Bold** from the **Text** menu

2   Type your name

3 Switch off the BOLD by clicking the **B** SmartIcon or by choosing **Bold** or **Normal** from the **Text** menu

Position the insertion point where you want to type the date

1 Switch on the ITALICS by clicking the *I* SmartIcon or by choosing **Italics** from the **Text** menu

2 Type in todays date

3 Switch off the ITALICS by clicking the *I* SmartIcon or by choosing **Italics** or **Normal** from the **Text** menu

Underline works exactly the same, but you click the underline <u>U</u> SmartIcon or choose **Underline** from the **Text** menu

In addition to Bold, Italics and Underline, other formatting options can be found in the Text Menu.

CAPS

<u>C</u>aps	<u>U</u>pper Case
Special E<u>ff</u>ects...	<u>L</u>ower Case
	<u>I</u>nitial Caps
	<u>S</u>mall Caps

The **Caps** option can be very useful for changing the case of existing text - particularly when you type in a heading in Uppercase, and discover yourself half way down the page, still in Uppercase!!

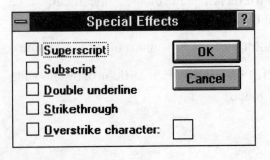

The **Special Effects** option opens a box with other effects to choose from.

Characters can have more than one formatting option applied to them - they may be bold, in italics and with double underline if your wish.

SELECTING TEXT USING CLICK AND DRAG

If the text you want to format already exists, you must **SELECT** the text before you switch on the formatting.

We will look at various selection techniques in the next section, but one method that works for any unit of text is **click and drag**.

To select text using this technique do the following (you might need to practise a little if you're not used to the mouse yet!).

1 Place the insertion point at the start of the text you want to select

2 Click and hold down the left mouse button

3 Drag along through the text until the desired selection is made

4 Let go the left mouse button

Should you select the wrong amount of text, point and click the left button anywhere within the text area to deselect it.

ENHANCING EXISTING TEXT

To enhance existing text:-

1 Select the text using the above technique (or any technique you know)

2 Click the appropriate SmartIcon for the formatting you want ie
B or *I* or <u>U</u>
OR
Choose the option desired from the **Text** menu

TO REMOVE FORMATTING FROM TEXT

Sometimes you'll find that you've formatting on text and then decide you want the text but not the formatting. Removing formatting and leaving the text is done in exactly the same way as adding formatting to existing text.

1   Select the text using the above technique (or any other)

2   Click the appropriate SmartIcon to remove the formatting you don't want ie **B** or *I* or <u>U</u>

     OR

     Choose from the **Text** menu

Doing the above REMOVES that formatting option from the text selected.

If text has a number of formatting options applied to it and you want to remove them all:

1   Select the Text

2   Choose **Normal** from the **Text** Menu

This removes all character formatting and returns the text to normal.

FAST FORMAT

If you've got text with formatting attributes you want to use on some other text you can use **Fast Format** to copy the formatting attributes over.

1   Select the text that has the formatting attributes you require

2   Click the **Fast Format** SmartIcon (or choose **Fast Format** from the **Text** menu)

3 The mouse pointer changes to a paint brush

4 Click and drag over the text you want to copy the formatting to

5 Let go the mouse button - the formatting is applied to the text you selected

When you don't want to Fast Format any more, click the SmartIcon again or switch it off using the Menu.

ALIGNMENT (Justification)

Alignment refers to the way the typing line is aligned between your margins. The options are left (the default), right, centre and justify.

Alignment	Left	^L
In**d**ention...	**C**entre	^E
Spacing...	**R**ight	^R
	Justify	^J

■ With **Left** Alignment each line is aligned with the LEFT margin and the right margin appears ragged.

■ With **Right** Alignment each line is aligned with the RIGHT margin and the left margin appears ragged.

■ With **Centre** Alignment each line is centred between the margins.

■ With **Justify** each line is flush with both the left and right margins (neither margin is ragged). To achieve this the spaces between the words in the line may be shrunk or stretched. Depending on the language you are using a Justified line can look a bit "gappy" - this is especially the case if there are a number of long words in it.

When you select an alignment option, that option remains in effect until you select another alignment option.

ALIGNING NEW TEXT

For example, let's say that you wanted to type a title at the top of your document, and that it was to be centred.

1 Place the insertion point at the beginning of your document

2 Press the **Enter** key to give yourself a blank line for your heading and move back into this blank line (so you've positioned yourself above any existing text)

3 Click the **CENTRE align** SmartIcon

4 The insertion point moves to the centre of the typing line

5 Type in your heading

6 Press **Enter**

The insertion point moves down a line and is still in the centre

If you wanted to type something in under the heading aligned to the left, you would have to click the **LEFT align** SmartIcon to send the insertion point back to the left margin.

You can move out of the centred area by moving your insertion point down into the body of your text.

In a NEW document, if you start by typing in a line or two of centred headings, you would:-

1 Select **Centre align**

2 Type the lines you to be centred

3 Select the alignment you need for the next section of your text, and continue typing

ALIGNING EXISTING TEXT

The alignment options are PARAGRAPH formatting options.

If text is already keyed in, you can place the insertion point anywhere in a paragraph and choose an alignment option. The paragraph containing the insertion point will take on that alignment.

Let's say you wanted to centre an existing paragraph.

1   Position the insertion point anywhere in the paragraph

2   Click the **Centre** SmartIcon.

The whole paragraph will be centred.

If you want to change the alignment of a number of consecutive paragraphs, or indeed the whole document, you must SELECT the paragraphs or the document first. (Clicking and dragging will do).

With the paragraphs selected, choose the appropriate alignment selection by clicking on the SmartIcon.

LINE SPACING

The documents you create using Ami Pro will be in single line spacing (6 lines to the inch) unless you specify otherwise.

The Line Spacing options are found in the **Text** menu, under **Spacing**.

TO SET LINE SPACING

1   Choose **Spacing** from the **Text** menu

The **Spacing** dialogue box appears

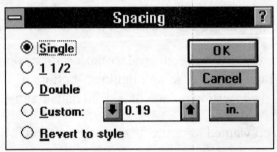

2 Complete as required - the options are **Single, 1½, Double, Custom** (where you can specify a non-standard spacing you require) or **Revert to style** (where the spacing of the style you are using will be selected - more on styles later).

At this stage you are likely to want one of the first 3.

3 Click the **OK** button to set the spacing.

Line Spacing is also a PARAGRAPH formatting command.

If you are entering new text, and set a line spacing command before you start typing, that line spacing will apply until you set another line spacing command.

If text is already typed up and you wish to change its line spacing you can either:

■ Place the insertion point in the paragraph you want to change the line spacing of, and choose from the **Spacing** dialogue box

   OR

■ Select the paragraphs you want to change the line spacing of (or select the whole document if you want to change the line spacing for the whole document) and then choose the spacing required from the **Spacing** dialogue box.

If you have been setting line spacing options and want to get back to the default spacing, choose **REVERT TO STYLE** from the Text, Spacing dialogue box.

■ If you'd like to practice these techniques, close your current document and open the one that you created in the last section.

TO OPEN AN EXISTING DOCUMENT

1 Click the **Open** SmartIcon or Choose **Open** from the **File** menu

The **Open** dialogue box appears.

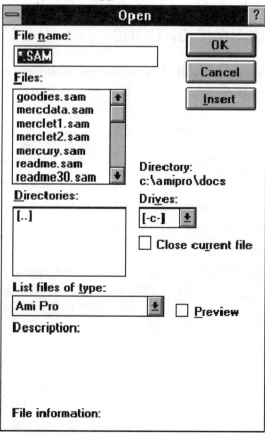

2 Change the **drive** and/or directory as necessary

3 In the **Files** box either type the name of the file required and click **OK** (or press **Enter**)

OR

Click the Filename required and then click **OK** (or press **Enter**)

OR

Double click the Filename

Try and edit your document as suggested.

RECAP ON SAVE OPTIONS

Once your document is edited as required you can save it using one of the techniques suggested in the previous section.

Remember, your options are:-

■ The **Save SmartIcon**, to save your document using the existing directory, path and filename

■ **Save** from the **File** Menu, to save your document using the existing directory, path and filename

■ **Save As** from the **File** Menu, so you can give your edited document a different directory, path or filename as required

The first two option have the same effect.

PLACES TO VISIT IN THE SCOTTISH BORDERS

There are many very interesting places to visit in the *Borders*. The area is very picturesque at any time of year with its hills, rivers, woods and historic towns.

There are many interesting towns and villages to visit. Some are quite industrial while others are very rural. The people in any of them will extend a warm welcome to visitors.

Places of particular interest include the **Abbeys** at Jedburgh, Kelso, Melrose, and Dryburgh, **Scott's View**, the **Lammermuir and Cheviot Hills**.

Another way to enhance your text is to change the style, size or colour of font. This can be done very easily by choosing **Font** from the **Text** Menu.

The **Font** dialogue box appears.

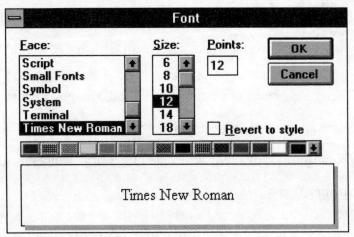

From the **Font** dialogue box you can change the font style, size or colour.

TO CHANGE FONT STYLE

Scroll up or down the vertical scroll bar in the **Face** box and click on the style you want.

A sample of the style you've selected will appear in the sample box in the lower section of the dialogue box.

TO CHANGE THE FONT SIZE

Scroll up or down the **Size** box until you reach the size you want, then click on it.

OR

Type the font size you require in the **Points** box (if it's not dimmed).

Font Styles, Sizes & Colour   8

TO CHANGE THE COLOUR OF YOUR FONT

(on screen only - it doesn't print out in colour unless you have a colour printer!).

Select the colour you want from the colour pallete.

STATUS BAR

You can also change the Font Style by clicking the **Face** button on the Status Bar and selecting the style from the list, or the Font Size by clicking the **Point Size** button on the Status Bar and selecting the size of character desired.

REVERT TO STYLE

If you've changed the Font Style, Size or Colour and want back to the default style for the paragraph, select the text, choose **Font** from the **Text** Menu, select the **Revert to Style** box then click **OK**.

SELECTING AND DE-SELECTING FONT STYLE, SIZE AND COLOUR

The techniques for switching these features on and off are the same as for the other character formatting commands; eg bold and underline.

You can select the features BEFORE you type the text, key in your text, then switch the features off again.

You can select text that has already been typed and select the font, size and/or colour required for the selected text.

You can select text that has already had font changes made to it and choose REVERT TO STYLE to go back to the default paragraph font settings.

■ Open your practice document and experiment with the Font options available.

9Selection & Keyboard Shortcuts

SELECTION TECHNIQUES

Now that you've started creating and editing documents with Ami Pro you'll have noticed that whenever you want to do something to EXISTING text you must SELECT the text first. Then you can format it as required, delete it, move it, copy it or type over it!

SELECT USING THE MOUSE

To help you SELECT text efficiently, here are some techniques you might want to practice as an alternative to the click and drag routine we've used so far.

To select:

a WORD	Double Click anywhere in the word
multiple WORDS	Double Click anywhere in the first word and DRAG
a SENTENCE	Hold the CTRL key down and click anywhere in the sentence
multiple SENTENCES	Hold CTRL, click and drag
a PARAGRAPH	Hold CTRL and Double Click
multiple PARAGRAPHS	Hold CTRL and double click and drag
large areas of text	Position the insertion point at the beginning to the text, move to the end of the text to be selected, hold down the SHIFT key and click.

BEWARE when text is selected, the **Enter**, **Backspace** or **Delete** key will delete the selected text, and pressing any alphanumeric key will REPLACE the selected text with what you type.

UNDO (the **SmartIcon** or **Edit, Undo**) will *usually* recover a selection you've deleted in error. I say *usually*, because the Undo levels must be set to at least 1 (you can have up to 4 levels of Undo, but the more levels you have the slower Ami Pro works). If you delete anything else in your panic it might overwrite the text you want to recover from the Undo buffer (this obviously depends on the number of levels you've set and the number of times you delete something). You can specify the number of Undo levels required in **Tools, User Setup**.

You can undo actions as well as deleted text, but Undo won't work if the document has been saved since you performed the action you want to undo. Some actions, eg Sort, can't be undone!

SELECT USING THE KEYBOARD

You can also select text using the keyboard. Position the insertion point at the beginning or the end of the text you want to select, hold the **Shift** key down, and use the cursor keys to move to the other end of the text to be selected . You can select text by holding down the **Shift** key and using any of the keyboard navigation techniques.

Try **Shift-Home** and **Shift-End** to select to the beginning or end of line from the insertion point.

Try **Shift-Ctrl-End** to select from the insertion point to the end of the document.

9 Selection & Keyboard Shortcuts

As you become accustomed to using Ami Pro you'll discover there is often more than one way to do everything! All the Ami Pro functions and features are available through the Menus. In addition to this, you are now aware that many of the more commonly used features can be accessed via the SmartIcons and the Status Bar.

KEYBOARD SHORTCUTS

If you're skillful on the keyboard however, you may find it a bit of a bind to have to continually remove your hands from the keyboard to use the mouse to click on the features you want, particularly when you're keying in a lot of text.

Many commonly used commands have keyboard shortcuts you can use. In the menus, the keyboard shortcuts for the options that have them are listed down the right hand side of the box. You will gradually learn the ones that you use most often. Most of the keyboard shortcuts are initiated by holding down the **Ctrl** key and pressing a letter or key on the keyboard (^ means hold the **Ctrl** key down).

Here's a full list of the shortcuts (we haven't covered them all yet!).

You don't HAVE to use keyboard shortcuts to do anything, but some of you may find them very convenient.

Selection & Keyboard Shortcuts 9

To do this	Use
Access Styles Box	^Y
Bold	^B
Centre Align	^C
Copy	^INS or ^C
Cut	SHIFT+DEL or ^X
Delete Next Word	^DEL
Delete Previous Word	^BACKSPACE
Draft/Layout View	^M
Exchange selected paragraph with the one above	ALT+ñ
Exchange selected paragraph with the one below	ALT+ò
Fast Format	^T
Find & Replace	^F
Full page/previous layout view	^D
Go To Dialogue Box	^G
>Go to Next Item	^H
Insert Glossary Record	^K
Italic	^I
Justify	^J
Left Align	^L
Modify Paragraph Style	^A
Normal Text	^N
Open Document	^O
Paste	SHIFT+INS or ^V
Print	^P
Right Align	^R
Save	^S
Show/Hide SmartIcons	^Q
Underline	^U
Undo	ALT+BACKSPACE or ^Z
Word underline	^W

When creating and editing documents you'll often find yourself rearranging your text as you decide a sentence, paragraph, or indeed any unit of text, would be better in another place.

You can do this quite simply, WITHOUT RETYPING THE TEXT, by using Cut or Copy and Paste techniques.

CUT, COPY AND PASTE WITHIN THE SAME DOCUMENT

CUT TEXT

When you **CUT** text, you remove it from its current position. You don't have to **PASTE** text that has been cut, but usually you will. (If you wanted the text deleted you'd have used a Delete command rather than a Cut one).

The reason you cut text is so that you can move it somewhere else - either in the same document or to a different one.

To cut text:

1 First you have to SELECT the text you want to cut. Then you do one of the following:-

2 Click the **Scissors** SmartIcon

OR

Choose **Cut** from the **Edit** menu

OR

Use the Keyboard shortcut **Shift-Delete** or **^X**

The selected text will disappear from your screen and is placed in the Clipboard. The Clipboard is a temporary storage location you can use when you move or copy text.

PASTE TEXT

To retrieve text from the Clipboard, you PASTE it into your document. To Paste text:

1 Position the insertion point where you want the text pasted in and do one of the following:

2 Click the **Paste** SmartIcon

OR

Choose **Paste** from the **Edit** menu

OR

Use the Keyboard shortcut **Shift-Insert** or ^**V**

The text from the clipboard is inserted at the insertion point.

COPY TEXT

If you want to take a COPY of text, ie leave the original text where it is but take a copy of it to insert somewhere else, you can do so using a very similar technique to CUT.

1 Select the text you want to copy and do one of the following:

2 Click the **Copy** SmartIcon

OR

Choose **Copy** from the **Edit** menu

OR

Use the Keyboard shortcut **Ctrl-Insert** or ^**C**

A copy of the selected text is put in the Clipboard.

3 You can then position your insertion point where you want the Copy of the text to appear, and PASTE it in as above.

Text is NOT removed from the Clipboard when it is pasted. When the next selection is Copied or Cut to the Clipboard, the old contents are overwritten. When you exit Windows, the Clipboard is cleared.

DRAG AND DROP

Another technique you might want to try, particularly for moving or copying over short distances, is Drag and Drop.

1   Select the text to be moved or copied

2   To MOVE text, **click** and **hold down** the left mouse button,
OR
to COPY text, hold the **Ctrl** key down while you **click** and **hold down** the left mouse button .

3   **DRAG** the insertion point to where you want to PASTE the text.

■   Notice that the mouse pointer has the **cut** or **copy** icon at its tail (depending on which function you choose) and a vertical insertion point at its nose. Watch the vertical bar until it is in the position you want to PASTE to.

4   **DROP** by letting go the left mouse button. The selected text will have been moved or copied to the insertion point.

CUT, COPY AND PASTE TO ANOTHER DOCUMENT

This is really no different to Cut, Copy and Paste within a document, with the exception that you have to OPEN the document you want to Paste into.

■ You can have a number of documents open at the same time in a Windows environment. To move from one window to another you simply click on any part of the window if it's visible or you can open the **Window** menu and choose the document name you want from the list.

To Cut or Copy to another Document do the following:-

1 Select the text you want to Cut or Copy

2 Cut or Copy the selected text

3 If the document you want to Paste to is not open, Open the document

4 Make the window that contains the document you want to Paste to the Active window

5 Position the insertion point where you want to Paste the text in the other document

6 Paste the text

Note: You can Open the receiving document at any time before you go to PASTE the text.

Open your practice document and try making the amendments shown overleaf, using CUT, COPY AND PASTE.

<u>PLACES TO VISIT IN THE SCOTTISH BORDERS</u>

There are many very interesting places to visit in the<u>Borders</u>. There are many interesting towns and villages to visit. Some are quite industrial while others are very rural. The people in any of them will extend a *warm welcome* to visitors.

Places of particular interest include the **Abbeys** at Jedburgh, Kelso, Melrose, and Dryburgh, **Scott's View, the Lammermuir and Cheviot Hills**.

The area is very picturesque at any time of year with its hills, rivers, woods and historic towns.

<u>PLACES TO VISIT IN THE SCOTTISH BORDERS</u>

You can determine exactly how and where on the page your text is to lie by using Margins, Tabs and Indents.

Margins control the amount of space between the text and the edge of the paper - there's a Top, Bottom, Left and Right Margin.

Tabs let you align your text at a particular position horizontally on the typing line - you might need to type up a list of names and phone numbers - you can use tabs to align each column.

Sometimes you don't require a paragraph to go out to the left and/ or right margins - you might want a quotation indented so it stands out clearly. You can use **Indents** to do this.

RULER

For most of your Margin, Tab and Indent work you'll be able to use the RULER.

■ Click the **Ruler** SmartIcon to display the ruler along the top of your screen or choose **View,Ruler Show**.

LEFT & RIGHT MARGINS

The lower half of the ruler indicates your left and right margin positions. They're indicated by the black triangles pointing in to the typing line. The default margins are set to 1" - to give a typing line of about 6.25" on standard A4 portrait paper.

To change the left or right margin, simply click and drag the margin indicators along the ruler until they are where you want them. Changing the margins in this way affects the WHOLE DOCUMENT.

To return the insertion point to the text area, point and click with the mouse, or press the **Esc** key.

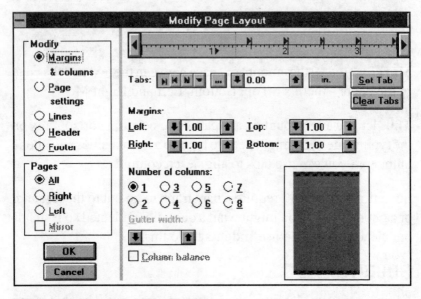

TOP & BOTTOM MARGINS

To change the Top and/or Bottom Margins, you have to go into **Page,Insert Page Layout** (if you want to change the page layout for *part* of your document only, starting at the top of the next page) or **Page,Modify Page Layout** (if you want to change the page layout for *all* of your document).

With the **Margins & Columns** option selected you can change the Left, Right, Top & Bottom margins for your page.

TABS

The upper half of the ruler shows the pre-set tab positions. They are set every half inch along the typing line and are LEFT tabs.

To edit the tab positions, click anywhere on the ruler to get the tab dialogue line displayed.

To clear all the pre-set tabs, click the **Clear Tabs** button.

To set your own tabs, click the tab type you want LEFT, RIGHT, DECIMAL or CENTRE (buttons at the left side of the tab dialogue line). Then click on the upper half of the ruler at the position you want to set the tab.

To delete an individual tab, click and drag it down, off the ruler.

LEADER DOTS

If you want a tab to have Leader Dots, select the tab type you want (left, right, decimal or centre), click the leader dot button (next button to the right) until the style of leader dot you want is displayed above the tab type buttons. Then set the tab in the desired position. The leader dot character is displayed in the tab set indicator on the ruler to show this tab has a leader dot.

You can also go into **Page,Insert Page Layout** or **Page,Modify Page Layout** and set your tabs when the **Margins & Columns** option is selected.

INDENTS

Indents allow you to bring the left or right edge of a paragraph in from the margins.

The indents are displayed at the left and right sides in the upper half of the ruler. There are 2 left indent markers so you can indent just the first line of a paragraph, all lines except the first line of a paragraph or all lines of a paragraph from the left margin.

There is one right indent marker so you can indent the right edge of your paragraph from the right margin if you want.

To move the indent markers, click and drag them along the ruler.

⌐⌐⌐ **To indent just the first line** of a paragraph from the left margin, click and drag the UPPER indent marker at the left edge of the ruler.

To indent all lines EXCEPT the first line of a paragraph from the left margin, click and drag the LOWER indent marker at the left edge of the ruler.

To indent all lines in the paragraph from the left margin, click and drag BOTH indent markers from the left edge of the ruler - point to the vertical line to the left of them to do this.

To indent from the right margin, click and drag the right indent marker to the desired position.

If you prefer you can choose **Text,Indention** to indent your paragraphs. The **Indention** dialogue box is displayed and you can complete it as you wish.

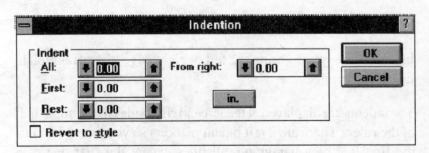

-3-
Proofing Tools

There are a number of useful tools for proofing your documents -
the Spell Check, Grammar Check and Thesaurus. This section and
the next 2 take you through these Tools.

Beware that Spell Checks ARE NOT foolproof - a correctly spelt
word in the wrong context is overlooked. If you get your "there"
and "their" mixed up, spell check won't help you put them right.
Spell checks can be very useful for picking up character transposi-
tion - "hte" instead of "the" - but beware, an "alter" instead of a
"later" will go undetected!!

Take a few minutes to appreciate how Ami Pro structures your
document into Text Streams - this way you'll understand better how
the Spell Checker and Grammar Checker work.

TEXT STREAMS

Ami Pro organises documents into portions of connected text called
TEXT STREAMS.

Text Streams have an order of priority:-

1   Main Document Text;

2   Text in Fixed Frames;

3   Footnote Text;

4   Text in Floating Frames;

5   Floating Header/Footer Text;

6   Fixed Header/Footer Text

(any of these "streams" you don't understand will become clearer
when you cover the relevant section of the book).

You can specify the text you want Spell or Grammar check to look
through by ensuring the insertion point is in the right kind of text
stream when you start.

If **Include other text streams** is selected (an option that is available in both **Spell** and **Grammar** dialogue boxes) then all lower priority text streams will be checked. If it isn't selected, then just the Text Stream the insertion point is in will be checked. If EVERYTHING has to be checked, make sure you're in the Main Document Text.

If you're NOT in the main document text stream when you start checking, Ami Pro dims the **Include other Text Streams** Option, and starts checking from the beginning of the document regardless of where the insertion point is.

Neither Spell nor Grammar Check examine Notes or Draw Frames.

You can SELECT text before you Spell or Grammar check - the check is then limited to the selected text.

SPELL CHECK

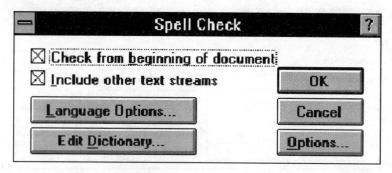

To Spell Check your document

1 Choose **Spell** from the **Tools** Menu (or click the **abc** SmartIcon).

2 Complete the dialogue box as required

3 Click **OK**

If the **Check from beginning of document** is selected, then the spell check begins from the beginning of the document regardless of where the insertion point is.

Include other text streams - if this is selected frames, headers, footers, footnotes etc will all be spell checked at the same time.

If you don't want to spell check the main document, but just the frames or headers/footers for example, make sure the insertion point is in the appropriate kind of text stream before you start.

To spell check just a word, or part of your document, select the text to be checked before going into Spell Check.

Ami Pro's main dictionary has 115,000 words in it.

When a spelling error is found the dialogue box below appears.

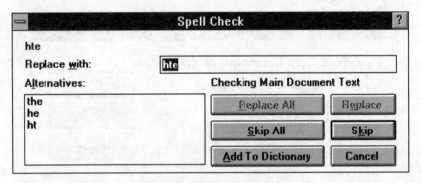

TO CHANGE A WRONG SPELLING

1   Click on the correct spelling from the list of **Alternatives**
    OR
    Type in the correct spelling in the **Replace with** field

2   Click **Replace All** or **Replace** as appropriate

IF IT'S NOT A WRONG SPELLING

The spell check may have stopped at a postcode or an abbreviation it doesn't recognise.

If you don't want to change it, or add it to the user Dictionary, click on **Skip All** or **Skip** and the system will leave it as it is.

TO ADD A WORD TO THE USER DICTIONARY

If the spell check has stopped at a correctly spelt word, you can add the word to the user dictionary so that it's not picked up as an error by the system again. Place names, company names and specialist vocabulary will need to be added.

Click **Add to Dictionary** to do this.

(If you work in Scotland you'll find MacPherson, MacDuff, MacDonald, Milngavie, Auchtermuchty etc picked up as errors by the system!! Just add them to the dictionary.)

TO EDIT THE USER DICTIONARY

Ami Pro has 2 dictionaries - the main one that you can't edit (with its 115,000 words) and the USER DICTIONARY. The User Dictionary is the one any words you **Add to Dictionary** during the spell check, go to.

You can edit the user dictionary by choosing **Edit Dictionary** from the **Spell Check** dialogue box. (If you discover you've added a wrongly spelt word to the dictionary, then you can use **Edit Dictionary** to DELETE the word. You can also ADD words directly to your dictionary).

The **Ami Pro User Dictionary** is displayed in a separate window.

To ADD a word

Type in the word, and press **Enter** (NB each word MUST be on a separate line and MUST have a carriage return after it). It doesn't matter where in the list you add your word - Ami Pro sorts them automatically.

The order Ami Pro lists the contents of the User Dictionary is:-

    Numbers;

    Symbols (in the order of the ANSI character set);

    Capitalised Words in alphabetical order;

    Lower Case Words in alphabetical order.

To DELETE a word

Select the word and the return at the end of its line. Press **Delete**.

To SAVE the changes

Make sure the User Dictionary is in the active window and choose **File,Save**.

To CLOSE the User Dictionary

Make sure the User Dictionary is in the active window and choose **File,Close**.

To check the grammar of your document choose **Grammar Check** from the **Tools** Menu (or click the **Grammar Check** SmartIcon).

In the dialogue box, select the grammar style you want to use and select the **Preferences** options you want.

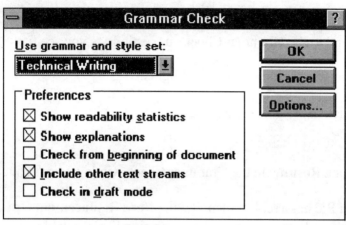

Show Readability Statistics - if you select this option Ami Pro provides data on the contents of your document at the end of the grammar check - details of the number of words, sentences, paragraphs, syllables and the averages for words and sentences among other things!

Show Explanations - when this is selected Ami Pro tells you why it's picked you up on your grammar and suggests what should be done to remedy things.

Check in Draft Mode - select this option if the document contains sentences that span columns or pages. Grammar Check can only display such sentences in their entirety in Draft mode.

Click **OK** to start the Grammar Check.

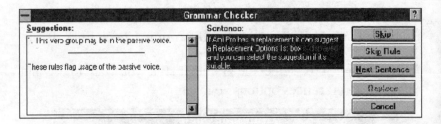

Respond to the Grammar Check suggestions as you see fit.

To change an error Ami Pro highlights:

1   Click in the document window

2   Make the change

3   Click **Resume** in the Grammar Check window to continue.

If Ami Pro has a replacement it will offer a **Replacement Options** list box, and you can select the suggestion if it's suitable.

Grammar Check Controls

Skip skips the occurrence of the error

Skip Rule skips all occurrences of the same kind of error during the current check

Next Sentence checks the next sentence, even if there are still grammatical errors in the current one.

Replace replaces the current sentence with the one you've selected from the replacement list box.

At the end of the Grammar Check the insertion point is in the last sentence that Ami Pro found an error in.

Readability Statistics

If you selected **Show Readability Statistics**, Ami Pro provides information about the contents and readability of your document.

Gunning's Fog Index indicates how difficult your document is to read - the *higher* the index the *harder* your document is to read.

Flesch-Kincaid Score - The *higher* the score, the *harder* your document is to read.

Flesch Reading Ease Score - The *higher* the score, the *easier* your document is to read and understand (highest score 100). An average score is between 60-70. 0-30 means your document is pretty hard to read and understand!

Flesch Reading Ease Grade Level - Translates the above to an American Grade level (Grade 1 = 6 Years Old).

To modify the rules for a grammar and styles set.

1 Choose **Options** from the **Grammar** dialogue box

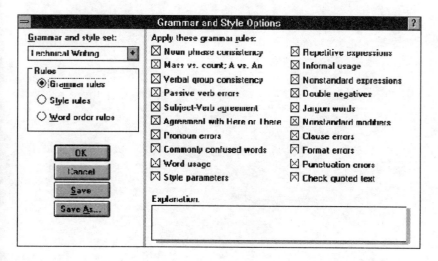

2   Select the **Grammar** and **Styles** set you want to modify

3   Select the type of **Rules** you want to modify

4   Select the **Rules** you want to **apply**

5   Click **OK**

NB Saving Grammar and Style Options

Save - Saves the new rules you've selected without closing the **Grammar and Style** options box. This way you can modify more than one set of rules at a time.

BEWARE - if you choose SAVE and modify the options provided with Ami Pro - you can't revert back the to defaults!!!

Use **Save As** to save your customised set of rules under a different name, and keep the original set.

The Thesaurus gives you access to alternative words and meanings of words in your documents - you can save yourself becoming too repetitive by finding an alternative through the Thesaurus.

If you want to look up an alternative to a word you've got in your document, put the insertion point inside the word and click the **Thesaurus** SmartIcon (or choose **Tools, Thesaurus**).

The **Thesaurus** dialogue box appears with suggested meanings and synonyms for the word selected.

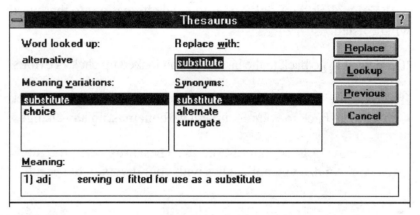

The **Meaning variations** list gives the various meanings of the word you've looked up.

The **Synonyms** list gives synonyms for the word selected in the **Meaning variations** list.

Choosing a different **Meaning variation** option produces a different list of Synonyms.

The **Meaning** field at the bottom gives an explanation of the term selected in the **Meaning variations** list.

If the word in the **Replace with** field is acceptable, click the **Replace** button and the word in your document will be replaced by the word in the **Replace with** field.

If you don't like the suggested replacement, but see another word in the lists that appeals to you, clicking that word places it in the **Replace with** field, and you can then click **Replace** to swap it with the word in your document.

If you want to look for other alternatives to the word in the **Replace with** field, click the **Look up** button and alternatives to that word will be listed.

If you want to go back to the last word you looked up click **Previous**.

If you decide that you used the best word in the first place, click **Cancel** to go back to your document without making any changes.

You can have a good jaunt round the Thesaurus when the mood takes you. Amaze you colleagues with your diversity of speech.

- 4 -
Beyond the Basics

Before going much further, you might want to consider the various options for VIEWING your document on the screen.

The way you view your document on the screen is primarily determined by the task you are doing, but there is room for personal taste too!

VIEW

There's a choice of 5 views that you can have of your document - Full Page, Custom %, Standard, Enlarged and Facing Pages.

FULL PAGE

This reduces the page so you can see the full page on the screen. You can only use this option in Layout mode.

You need to have pretty good eyesight to read anything in full view but it's useful for letting you see the pattern of text and pictures. You can edit the page when in this view. Use the **View Full Page, Layout View** icon on the toolbar to go in and out of this view.

CUSTOM %

You can specify how much of the page should be displayed using this option. **Standard** view is the same as 100%. **Enlarged** view is the same as 200%. Ami Pros custom default is 91% (this is 91% of Standard view). You can specify anything from 10-400%.

Choose **View, View Preferences** to specify the % view you have.

STANDARD

This shows the page in the same size as other Microsoft Windows applications. You might need to use the horizontal scrollbar to see the beginning and end of each line.

ENLARGED

Useful for getting a close up on certain areas. It's twice the size of standard view.

FACING PAGES

A useful option for viewing documents to be bound with facing pages - you can see what the pages will look like side by side. You can't edit in this view.

DISPLAY MODES

There are 3 display modes - Layout, Outline and Draft.

LAYOUT MODE

This gives you a WYSIWYG (What You See Is What You Get) appearance. The document appears as it will print with type style, size and formatting all displayed on screen. The text, pictures, headers, footers, footnotes and tables all appear in the document.

OUTLINE MODE

This gives you a collapsible/expandable structured view of your document. We'll look at this view in more detail when we look at Outlining.

DRAFT MODE

This mode provides a less formatted view of your document than Layout mode. Page breaks, headers, footers and footnotes are not displayed.

Tables and text or pictures in anchored frames display in the correct place in the document but text or pictures in other types of frames don't appear at all.

DISPLAYING PARTS OF THE WINDOW

SHOW/HIDE SMARTICONS

You can toggle the display of the SmartIcons using **Ctrl-Q** or by using the **Hide/Show SmartIcons** option on the **View** menu. You can also use the **SmartIcons** button on the **Status Bar** for this.

SHOW/HIDE CLEAN SCREEN

You may be one of those people who find all the toolbars, menus and scroll bars take up too much room when displayed all the time. You might want to display more of your document on screen and fewer "accessories".

There is a Clean Screen option just for you!

Before choosing **Show Clean Screen** from the **View** menu, have a look and see what options you have.

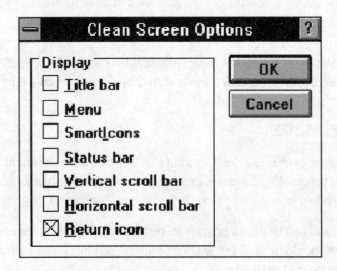

1   Choose **View, View Preferences..., Clean Screen Options...**

The **Clean Screen Options** dialogue box appears.

2   Check the screen elements that you want to display when you choose the **Clean Screen** option.

(The **Return** Icon one is useful even if you don't want to display anything else - to get back from your clean screen view to your normal view you just click the icon.)

3   Click **OK**.

When you choose **View, Show Clean Screen** only the elements indicated in the Options box will be displayed.

(If you clear EVERYTHING off the screen you can use **Alt-V** to display the view menu again)

SHOW/HIDE RULER

Use the **View, Show/Hide ruler** option or the **Show/Hide ruler** icon on the toolbar to toggle the ruler display.

SHOW/HIDE STYLES BOX

You can toggle the display of the Styles box using the **View, Show/Hide styles** box option.

SHOW/HIDE POWER FIELDS

You can toggle the display of Power Fields by using the **View, Show/Hide Power Fields** option. (Some of the more advanced features use Power Fields - don't worry about them yet!).

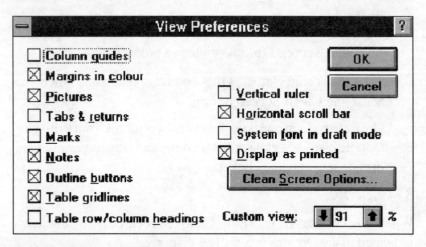

VIEW PREFERENCES

You can set up your own View Preferences through the **View, View Preferences** option.

Check the boxes to specify the options you want to view on screen and click **OK**.

VIEWING MULTIPLE DOCUMENTS

You can have up to 9 documents open in Ami Pro at any one time.

To open a number of documents use the **File, Open ...** for each one but make sure you de-select the **Close Current File** box!

When you've got more than one file open, you can make a different file the active window by choosing its name from the **Window** menu.

If you want to view more than one document at a time on the screen, choose **Window, Tile** - each document is displayed in a smaller window so that all documents can be seen at once.

You can display the windows so that the documents overlap by choosing **Window, Cascade**. The Title Bar of each window is visible with the active window on top.

There will be times when you want your work presented in a number of COLUMNS rather than in a single column running from left to right margin.

Depending on the type of columnar work that you're doing, you'll either use the **COLUMNS** or the **TABLES** feature in Ami Pro.

This section describes how to use the COLUMNS feature. The columns feature lets you produce work in NEWSPAPER style columns, where the text runs from top to bottom of the first column and then wraps into the second column, runs from top to bottom of the second column and then wraps into the third column and so on.

You can have up to 8 columns in Ami Pro.

PAGE LAYOUT

Columns are a PAGE LAYOUT feature (like margins). When you set columns they apply to all pages (if you want to have apparently different page layouts on the same page you must use Frames).

MODIFY PAGE LAYOUT VS INSERT PAGE LAYOUT

■ When you use **Modify Page Layout**, to change your margins or columns, the layout of the whole document is affected, regardless of where your insertion point is when you give the command.

■ When you use **Insert Page Layout** with margins or columns, the new page layout starts at the beginning of the next page, and changes the document layout from there on down (unless it encounters another Page Layout command).

SETTING UP COLUMNS

The easiest way to set up your columns is using the ruler.

1   Click on the ruler to display the tab dialogue line.

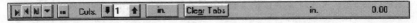

2   Edit the **Cols** field to show the number of columns you require (use either the up/down arrows at each side of the field or simply type in the number of columns you want).

Each column will be of equal width and the gutter margins (the margins between the columns) will be of equal width.

3   Point and click to position the insertion point back in the main text (or press **Esc**).

CHANGING THE WIDTH OF COLUMNS OR GUTTERS

(Gutters are the margins between columns)

Simply click and drag the column markers on the ruler. This way you can customise the columns widths and gutters to suit your requirements.

Alternatively, you can choose **Page, Insert Page Layout** or **Page,Modify Page Layout** and set up your columns there. (You can't set unequal gutters in the dialogue box).

COLUMN BALANCING

With each page that is completed Ami Pro automatically balances the columns as far as it can - this means each column will finish on the same line (if possible).

If your columns don't fill the whole page, you can select the **Column Balancing** checkbox in the **Modify Page Layout** dialogue box, and Ami Pro will redistribute the text evenly between the columns so that each column contains about the same amount of text - ie you don't end up with column 1 and 2 filled, and nothing in column 3.

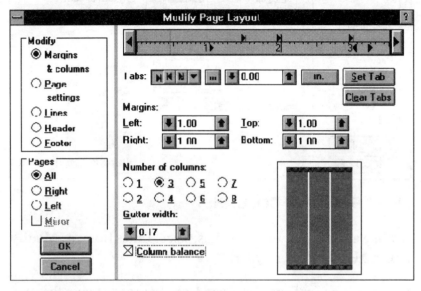

TYPING TEXT IN COLUMNS

As you key in your text, you complete one column before you are automatically wrapped up to the beginning of the next. At the end of the last column you are automatically wrapped onto the first column of a new page.

MANUAL COLUMN BREAK

If you need to force a column break you can choose the **Page, Breaks...** option and select **Insert Column Break**.

If you insert a Manual Column Break in the last column, you're taken to the next page.

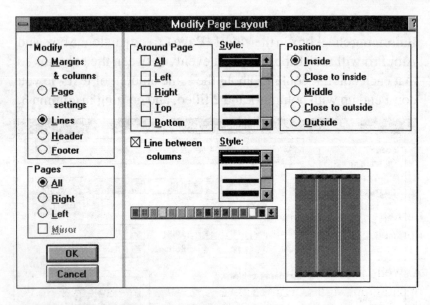

LINES BETWEEN COLUMNS

If you want lines between columns, select **Lines** from the **Modify** box in **Modify Page Layout**.

Select the box for **Lines Between Columns**, and choose the style and colour of line as required.

Now that you're familiar with page, paragraph and character formatting let's consider using STYLES. Styles are simply recorded formatting instructions, and although we've not mentioned it before, you've been using Styles since you started using Ami Pro!

Every new document you create in Ami Pro is based on a STYLE SHEET. The style sheet most often used (and the one we've used up till now) is the default one (_DEFAULT.STY). A style sheet is simply a template, or a pattern, on which to base your document. Once you've selected a style sheet you can use it as it is or change the margins, tabs, number of columns, font, alignment etc (as you've done up until now) to suit your document.

As well as a Page Layout, a style sheet gives you access to a number of paragraph styles. You've always used the paragraph style Body Text (see style button on status bar). If you've wanted to change the alignment, tabs, indents, or character formatting of your paragraph, you've used the menus, SmartIcons or keyboard shortcuts. There is nothing to stop you continuing to do so, but there are a number of advantages in using Styles. The two main ones are SPEED and CONSISTENCY.

Imagine you're working on a report that has a main heading (perhaps centred, bold, point size 18), section headings (perhaps left aligned, bold, underlined, point size 14) and you want the body text as is. You could format each heading manually each time it's needed OR you could format each heading ONCE, then save the formatting instructions as a STYLE and apply that STYLE when you need it. Much quicker! You also eliminate the risk of forgetting exactly how you formatted - did you underline the previous heading or not?? So it's consistent.

Once your report is complete, you might decide that you don't like
the bold and underline together, and want to remove the underline.
If you use a Style, all you need to do is edit the style and all text within
your document that has the style applied to it is automatically
updated. Again, it's much quicker than going to each heading and
changing the formatting manually!

To summarise:-

A Style Sheet consists of:- *one* page layout

a number of paragraph styles.

The main benefits of using styles are:- Speed

Consistency

Let's look at the Style Sheet you've been using a bit closer. Look
at the **New File** dialogue box first.

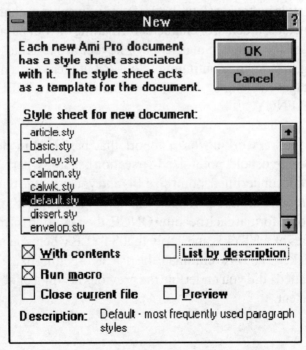

SELECTING A STYLE SHEET

You can't create a document without first selecting a Style Sheet to base it on. The document you create has the Page layout and Paragraph styles of the Style Sheet you've selected. When you choose **File, New** the **New File** dialogue box lists the Style Sheets available to you. You may have the style file names (_DEFAULT.STY) or the style description listed depending on whether the **List By Description** box is selected or de-selected.

SELECTING WITH CONTENTS

This means that the Style Sheet you've selected will include text, frames, pictures or tables from the template (provided it has some).

When you select a Style Sheet like _DEFAULT.STY which has no text, frames, pictures or tables, the **With contents** option has no effect because there are no contents to display.

SELECTING RUN MACRO

If you select this option, then Ami Pro prompts you for any default information that's required for the type of document you're about to create. For example with _LETTER1.STY you're asked for details of the sender's name, title, your company, address, etc - this information is then automatically inserted into the appropriate bit of the document.

Once the default information is complete, you are prompted to give optional information. Again, Ami Pro automatically inserts this information in the appropriate place in the document.

When you select a Style Sheet like _DEFAULT.STY which has no macro, the **Run macro** option has no effect.

SELECTING CLOSE CURRENT FILE

This option will close any file that is open before creating a new one.

SELECTING LIST BY DESCRIPTION

Selecting this option lists the Style Sheet description in the Style Sheet list box, instead of the Style Sheet name.

SELECTING PREVIEW

Selecting this option lets you preview the style before you select it.

Ami Pro provides a number of Style Sheets ready for you to use. Alternatively, you can create your own customised one. Have a look through your Style Sheet Guide supplied with the package to see what you get. There might be something that's just what you need!

PARAGRAPH STYLES

Each style sheet has a number of paragraph styles - they vary from style sheet to style sheet. Clicking on the **Style** button on the Status Bar lists the paragraph styles that are part of your selected style sheet. (You could also choose **View, Show Styles Box** to display the styles box on your screen).

```
F2  Body Text
F3  Body Single
F4  Bullet
F5  Bullet 1
F6  Number List
F7  Subhead
F8  Title
F9  Header
F11 Footer
```

The ones listed here are in the _DEFAULT.STY

TO APPLY A PARAGRAPH STYLE

As with all formatting, you can either choose the paragraph style required before you key in the text, or you can apply a paragraph style to selected text.

1 Click on the **Style** button on the status bar to display the paragraph styles.

2 Choose the style required from the list given.

Try out the paragraph styles from the _DEFAULT.STY Style Sheet to see what's there.

In the next section we'll look at setting up your own styles and managing them.

18   Styles - Creating Your Own

CREATING YOUR OWN PARAGRAPH STYLES

Perhaps the easiest way to do this is:-

1 **Select** the text that has the paragraph formatting you want in a
   style (perhaps a heading you've just typed, centred, bold, point
   size 20, and red!).

2 Choose **Create Style** from the **Style** Menu

3 Give your style a name and in the **Based on** options, choose
   Selected text.

4 Click **Create**.

Alternatively you can:-

1 Choose **Create Style** from the **Style** Menu

2 Give your style a name

3 Choose the style it's **Based on** from the list

4 Click **Modify**

5 Make the required changes and click **OK**.

MODIFYING AN EXISTING PARAGRAPH STYLE

1 Choose **Modify** from the **Style** Menu

2 In the **Style** field, select the style you want to modify

3 Make the required modifications in the other fields

4 Click **Save** (to replace the existing style)
   OR
   Click **Save As** (to give your modified style a new name - this way
   the original stays too)

Styles - Creating Your Own   18

TO REDEFINE AN EXISTING STYLE

1   Place the insertion point within the paragraph that has the formatting that you want to re-define the current style to.

2   Choose **Define** from the **Style** Menu

3   You will be prompted as to whether or not you want to change the attributes of the current paragraph style. Click **YES** or **NO** as required.

CREATING YOUR OWN STYLE SHEET

If you want to design your own Style Sheet for your reports, letters or memos this can be done quite easily.

1   Create a New File based on an existing Style Sheet (perhaps _DEFAULT.STY)

2   Set the Page Layout as required (Margins, number of columns, tabs, lines, header/footer details)

3   Create any paragraph styles for headings, hanging paragraphs, numbered lists, bulleted lists etc that you want to have as part of your Style Sheet.

4   Type in any standard text that should appear on all documents -in a memo this may be a heading eg*MEMORANDUM*, and the *To, From, Date, Subject* labels.

5   Choose **Save as a Style Sheet** from the **Style** Menu.

6   Give the Style a name (_MYMEMO.STY)

7   Complete the **Description, With Contents, Run Macro** as appropriate

8   Click **OK**

```
┌─────────────────────────────────────────────────────┐
│ ━       Save as a Style Sheet              ?         │
├─────────────────────────────────────────────────────┤
│ File name:      ┌─────────────────┐   ┌──────────┐   │
│                 │ _MYMEMO.STY     │   │    OK    │   │
│ Style sheet path:  c:\amipro\styles └──────────┘   │
│ Description:                          ┌──────────┐   │
│ ┌─────────────────────────────────┐   │  Cancel  │   │
│ │ Internal Memo Form              │   └──────────┘   │
│ │                                 │                  │
│ │                                 │                  │
│ └─────────────────────────────────┘                  │
│ ☒ With contents                                      │
│ ☐ Run macro:    ┌──────────────────────┐  ┌───┐     │
│                 │                      │  │ ↓ │     │
│                 └──────────────────────┘  └───┘     │
└─────────────────────────────────────────────────────┘
```

USING PARAGRAPH STYLES FROM OTHER STYLE SHEETS

If you need a paragraph style from a different Style Sheet

1 Choose **Use Another Style Sheet** from the **Style** menu

2 Select the Style Sheet you require from the list

3 Click **OK**

The paragraph styles belonging to the selected Style Sheet will be made available in your current document - you can click on the **Style** button in the status bar to check how the list has changed.

If you require paragraph styles from several different Style Sheets for your document

1 Choose **Use Another Style Sheet** from the **Style** menu

2 Select the Style Sheet you require from the list

3 Click **OK**

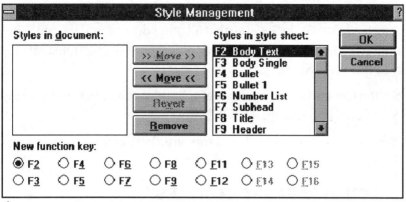

4   Choose **Style Management** from the **Style** menu

5   Move the styles you require to your document

6   Click **OK**

Repeat the steps above until you have all the required paragraph styles in your document

7   As a last step, choose **Use Another Style Sheet** from the **Style** menu and select the sheet that contains the PAGE LAYOUT for your document.

You should now have your document, with the page layout you require, and the paragraph styles needed.

STYLE MANAGEMENT

Standard paragraph styles belong to the Style Sheet used for your document. When you apply a standard style, Ami Pro finds the formatting instructions for that style in the STYLE SHEET.

However, if you've created or edited some styles while working on your document, the formatting for the new or modified style is attached to your DOCUMENT, not the Style Sheet.

18 Styles - Creating Your Own

If you've created or modified a paragraph style, and you want to attach it to the Style Sheet so that all other documents created using the Style Sheet have access to the paragraph style, you must MOVE it to the Style Sheet.

So, the formatting for your paragraph styles can be held either in the STYLE SHEET or the DOCUMENT.

You can move styles back and forwards between Style Sheets and documents using Style Management.

DELETING PARAGRAPH STYLES

You can delete a paragraph style from a document or Style Sheet by selecting it from the list and clicking the **Remove** button.

REVERT TO STANDARD STYLE

If you've modified a paragraph style in your document, and want to go back to the original formatting attributes in the Style Sheet, select the style from the **Styles in document** list and click **Revert**.

It's worth experimenting with styles - they can be great time savers!

THINGS TO REMEMBER WHEN USING STYLES

1   When you apply a standard style (one straight from the style sheet) the style remains in the Style Sheet

2   When you change a style, the changes only apply to the current document and the style name has a bullet beside it in the style box (eg you change the font size in the Title style).

3   When you change a style it moves to the **Style In Document** list in the **Style Management** dialogue box. The edited style affects paragraphs formatted with it within the current document only.

4   If you want paragraph styles from other Style Sheets choose **Use Another Style Sheet** from the **Style** menu and complete as required but note:-

If the new Style Sheet has the same style names as the current one, but with different settings, the document will take on the new formatting from the new Style Sheet.

5   If you want to keep any paragraph styles from the Style Sheet currently in use, but also access some from another Style Sheet, MOVE THE STYLES OVER TO THE **STYLE IN DOCUMENT** LIST before you **Use Another Style Sheet**

You can customise your document by pulling styles in from various style sheets as long as you remember the order:-

1   Move the required styles from the current Style Sheet over to the styles in document list if they're not already there (using **Style Management** in the **Style** menu)

2   Choose **Use Another Style Sheet** from the **Style** menu, select the style required and click **OK**

3   Move the required styles over into the **Style in document** list from the new Style Sheet

4   Choose **Use Another Style Sheet** from the **Style** menu

5   When all the paragraph styles required are in you document list, choose the style that contains the page layout for the document you are creating.

You can overwrite any style formatting using the SmartIcons, menus, buttons and keyboard shortcuts to format text (The way you've always done before we started looking at styles!).

Glossaries are a feature that those of you using standard clauses or paragraphs will love.

Even if you don't have a lot of the traditional "standard stuff", you'll find this feature useful for things like complimentary closes, circulation lists, opening phrases to your letters and so on.

Sales, legal and personnel environments that have a lot of "standard text" will find this feature extremely useful.

When using Glossaries you work with 2 files:

■ The Glossary data file that contains the standard text you'll be pulling in

and

■ The Document you're working on

There are 3 basic stages to setting up and using Glossaries:

1   Create, save and close the glossary data fil

2   Create a new file or open an existing file that you want to insert a Glossary record into

3   Establish the link between the 2 files and Insert the Glossary record at the desired place

Let's see how it works!

1 CREATE, SAVE & CLOSE THE GLOSSARY DATA FILE

Open a New file that is to become your Glossary Data File.

You must ensure that your Glossary Data File is of the required STRUCTURE so follow the next bit carefully!!

1 On the 1st line of the file, type in 2 *delimiters* (characters used to mark the end of something) with no space between them eg ~| or **#?**   The first character is the FIELD delimiter and the second one is the RECORD delimiter. (these 2 characters should NOT appear anywhere inside a data record - they should be unique)

2 Press **Enter**

3 On the 2nd line, type a FIELDNAME for the record IDs, which will be used to identify the glossary file records, followed by the Field Delimiter. Then type in a FIELDNAME for the DATA part of the glossary file records, followed by the Record Delimiter.

4 Press **Enter**

5 Then type in the first Record ID (your label for the first Glossary entry) followed by the Field Delimiter.
IMMEDIATELY after this, type in the DATA for the record - this can be anything from a phrase to several paragraphs.

6 Insert the RECORD delimiter at the end of the Data and press **Enter**.

7 Type in the Record ID for the next entry, followed by the Field Delimiter. Key in the Data. At the end, insert the Record delimiter and press **Enter**.

8 Continue doing this until all your Data Records are in.

9 When you're finished, save and close your file. (It's a good idea to call your Glossary file something like GLOSS.SAM so that it's easily identified from your other files.)

Read through the example below to see what your STRUCTURE should look like. I've used # as the FIELD delimiter, and I as the RECORD delimiter.

#|

RECORDID FIELD#RECORDTEXT FIELD|

ID for Record 1#Data for Record 1|

ID for Record 2#Data for Record 2|

ID for Record 3#Data for Record 3|

Here's an example of an actual Glossary Data File. You type the data in as you want it to appear when it's inserted into your document.

#|

RECID#RECTEXT|

open#Thank you for your enquiry about computer vacancies within our organisation. |

no#At the moment we are not actively looking for staff in this section. This situation is constantly changing so please do not hesitate to contact us again in the future. |

yesproject#We are not actively looking for permanent staff in this section at the moment. However, we are looking for one or two specialists to do contract work on a short term project. If you think you might be interested in this please contact |

contact1#Joe Jamieson on Ext 2424.|

contact2#Jennifer Robertson on Ext 2534.|

close#Yours sincerely

Pamela Jones

Recruitment Executive|

Ensure your Record IDs are unique. If you're using numbers to identify your records, each Record ID should have the same number of digits, ie 021, 123, 001

2 CREATE OR OPEN THE FILE YOU WANT TO INSERT A GLOSSARY ENTRY INTO

Once you've created your Glossary Data File you can insert entries from it into any Ami Pro document.

Create a New file or open an existing one in the normal way.

3 ESTABLISH A LINK BETWEEN THE TWO FILES AND INSERT GLOSSARY RECORDS

1 Position the insertion point where you want the glossary record to be inserted.

2 Choose **Edit, Insert, Glossary Record**. The **Insert Glossary Record** dialogue box appears.

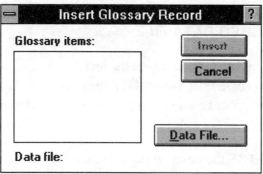

3 Choose **Data File....** The **Data File** dialogue box appears.

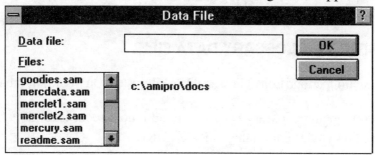

4 Select the drive and directory as require.

5 Specify the name of your Glossary Data File

6 Click **OK**

Once the link is established, the data record names are listed in the **Insert Glossary Record** dialogue box.

7 Choose the record name from the list and click **Insert**.

With the link between your document and data file established, you don't need to choose **Data File** from the **Insert Glossary Record** dialogue box again unless you want to change the Data File you're using.

SHORTCUTS FOR ENTERING DATA RECORDS FROM THE ATTACHED DATA FILE

■ Place the insertion point where the record is to appear and press **Ctrl-K** to access the **Insert Glossary Record** dialogue box, choose the record name from the list and click **Insert**.

OR

■ If you KNOW the name of the glossary record you want from the attached Data File you can insert the glossary record at the insertion point by typing in the name of the glossary record and then pressing **Ctrl-K**.

EDITING A GLOSSARY DATA FILE

You can Open and Edit a Glossary Data File just as you would any other.

If you Open a Glossary Data File to add more records to it, make sure that you maintain the STRUCTURE.

CREATING A GLOSSARY RECORD FROM SELECTED TEXT

If you've keyed text into your document and then decide it would make a useful Glossary record, you can add it to your Glossary Data File without re-keying it.

1 Select the text you want to become a Glossary Record

2 Choose **Edit, Mark Text, Glossary**

3 If the Data File you want to add the record to is not attached, choose **Data File...** select the desired Data File and click **OK**.

4 Type in an ID name for the Glossary Record.

5 Click **OK** to add the record and return to your document.

As you work with Ami Pro you might find that the default Setup is not the one you want to work with. If you're always changing the path when saving your documents, or you want to set an automatic backup, or edit the number of Undo levels (the higher you make this the slower Ami Pro works) you can do so by choosing **Tools, User Setup**.

The **User Setup** dialogue box appears for you to edit as necessary. Set the options required and click OK.

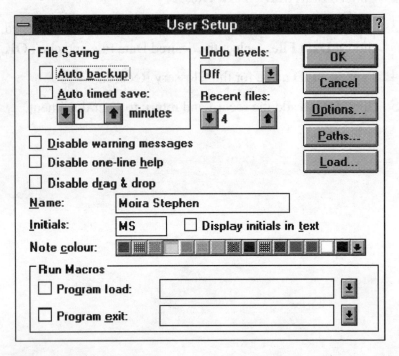

File Saving Options

If you select **Auto backup** in **File Saving**, Ami Pro will automatically create and save a copy of the original file (as it was before you edited it) before saving the updated version. The file will have the same name and extension as the one you are saving. It is therefore ESSENTIAL that you specify a Backup path that is different to the Document path in the **Default Paths** dialogue box (see below). If you don't, the backup copy is overwritten by the newly saved version.

If you select **Auto timed save** you can specify how often Ami Pro should automatically save your document for you.

Either option offers some security against your file being accidentally lost.

You can specify the number of **Undo levels** required, and the number of **Recent files** to be displayed in the File Menu. Use the on-line help to see what the other options do.

If you choose **Options...** from the **Setup** Window you can edit the **Typographic** or **Speed** options.

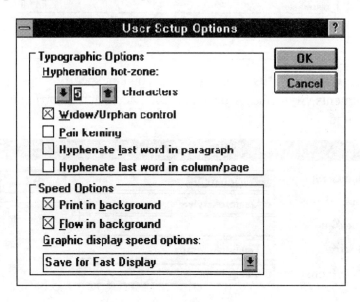

If you need to change your Load defaults (the default View, display
Mode and Style sheet) choose **Load...** from the **Setup** window and
edit the **Load Defaults** as necessary.

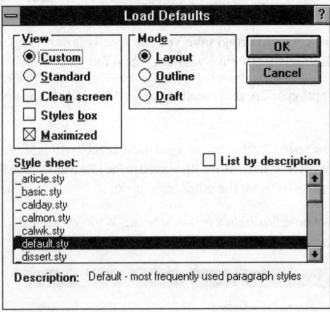

In the **Default Paths...** dialogue box you can specify where your
documents, Style Sheets, backup files, macros and SmartIcons can
be found.

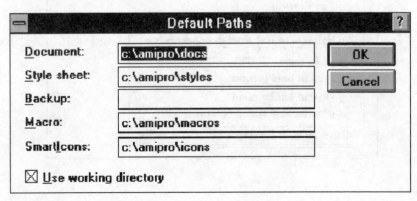

Once you've set up your defaults, you can edit them at any time as and when your circumstances change.

You can come out of Setup without making any changes by clicking the **Cancel** buttons.

Investigate the alternatives, listed in the various Setup dialogue boxes, using the context sensitive help from the appropriate Setup dialogue box.

SMARTICON SETS

So far we've used the DEFAULT SmartIcon set - the set that contains the icons most people want, most of the time!

VIEWING AND CHANGING SETS

You may, or may not, have noticed that there are other SmartIcon sets. Click the **SmartIcon** button on the Status Bar to see the list available. Just point and click at a set that interests you - the Editing set gives you speedy access to many of the functions and features we've looked at so far.

You can also travel through the list using the **Change SmartIcon** icon! Each time you click on it you move onto the next set in the list.

Have a look at what's there - you'll probably find that you would be better using different SmartIcon sets in different situations. Don't worry if some icons look unusual - Ami Pro does a lot of things and we're just getting into it!

If you choose a set, and don't know what some of the icons do, don't be shy - point and click to try them out.

CREATING YOUR OWN, CUSTOMISED SET

You can also generate your own, personal SmartIcon set that has all your favourites in it.

Choose **SmartIcons** from the **Tools** menu

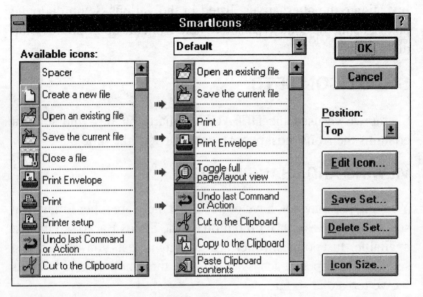

TO ADD ICONS TO YOUR SET

Click and drag the icons you want from the**Icons Available** list over into the **Set** list - drop them in the position that you want.

TO REMOVE ICONS FROM YOUR SET

Click and drag unwanted icons off the **Set** list.

TO SAVE YOUR ICON SET

Choose **Save As** and complete the dialogue box as required - if you want your set in addition to those supplied, use a unique file name. Ami Pro automatically gives an .SMI extension to SmartIcon Set files.

TO DELETE AN ICON SET

Choose **Delete Set** from the dialogue box. Select the set you want to delete from the list and click **OK**.

TO CHANGE THE SIZE OF SMARTICONS

Choose **Icon Size** from the dialogue box and complete as required.

- 5-
Powerful Features

These are brilliant! (Sorry for sounding a bit biased!).

Using Frames you can combine apparently different page layouts on the one page (you can have a section in 3 columns, and a heading spanning all three columns).

You can make text flow around frames, over frames or above and below frames. You can put notes into indents, tables, headers and footers using frames. You can place graphics in your document. Frames can be transparent (so you see through them) or opaque (so they hide what's behind them). You can give frames a line around them, or a shadow effect, or have no lines so that multiple frames can be layered and still look like one!

A frame is like a mini-document within a document - it can have text or a picture inside it - and it isn't affected by the formatting in the main document.

Try this - you'll love it!

CREATE A FRAME

1   To create a frame click the **Frame** icon on the toolbar.

2   Move the pointer down into the document and **click** and **drag** to draw the frame where you want it.

Don't worry if you make it the wrong size or put it in the wrong place - it's easy to fix!

Text can wrap around the frame as is the case here in the default frame.

FRAMES ARE EASY, VERSATILE, POWER-FUL AND FUN!

This frame has text above, below and to the right and left of it.

Once the frame is in your document it's easy to resize or move.

The DEFAULT frame, as above, is positioned "where placed" (ie it stays where it is unless you move it). It has a single line all around, rounded corners, a normal shadow and text is set to wrap around the frame. You'll see later how easy it is to specify your own frame design to suit your requirements.

TO RESIZE A FRAME

1 Click anywhere within the frame to **select** it - you know it's selected when there are black "handles" on each corner and along each side.

2 **Click** and **drag** on any of the handles to make the frame bigger or smaller. (The pointer changes to a double headed arrow when you're on the handle).

TO MOVE A FRAME

1 **Select** the Frame.

2 **Click** and **drag** with the pointer anywhere within the frame. (You get a broken line round the frame when you're moving it).

3 **Let go** the mouse button when you've moved the frame to where it should be.

TO KEY IN TEXT WITHIN A FRAME

1 **Double click** inside the Frame.

2 You can then key in any text required. If the frame is too big or too small for the text you want to key in, you'll have to resize it.

TO DE-SELECT A FRAME

1 **Click** anywhere **outside** the Frame.

Modify Frame Layout

Let's have a closer look at the **Modify Frame Layout** options.

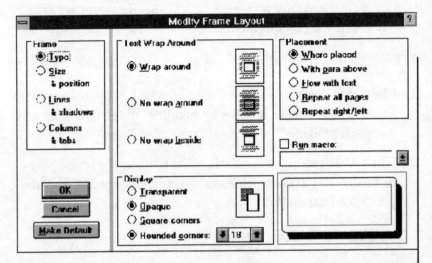

When you select a Frame and choose **Modify Frame Options** you get the dialogue box above. There's a choice of 4 frame options you can modify -**Type, Size & Position, Lines & Shadows** and **Columns & Tabs**.

TYPE

This option lets you specify how the text should wrap around the frame, where the frame should be placed within your document and how the frame should be displayed.

Text Wrap Around

Wrap Around lets text flow above, below and to the right and left of the frame.

No Wrap Around lets the text flow above, below and through the frame - with the Display option set to **Transparent** you'd be able to see the text; with **Opaque**, the text behind the frame would be hidden.

No Wrap Beside lets the text flow above and below the frame only.

Placement

This lets you determine where in the document you want the frame to be. If **Where placed** is selected the frame remains where you put it regardless of any text editing that goes on in the main document around it.

You can ANCHOR your frame using the **With Para Above** or the **Flow With Text** options. A frame anchored **With Para Above** is attached to the return at the end of a paragraph in the main document. A frame anchored in this way can be moved horizontally, but NOT vertically.

If you anchor your frame using the **Flow With Text** option the frame is anchored to the last character within a paragraph of the main document. The frame moves as you insert or delete text within the paragraph. You can move a frame anchored in this way vertically but NOT horizontally.

With anchored frames, the frames can't be any wider than the column whose text they're attached to and no deeper than the amount of space left in the column or page.

Repeat All Pages repeats the frame and its contents in the same place on every page.

Repeat Right/Left repeats the frame and its contents in the same place on alternate pages (right are ODD, left are EVEN pages).

■   The best way to get a feel for this is to experiment with the options; watch the sample box in the bottom right hand corner to see the effect on the frame, and move back to your document to see the effect on **Text wrap** and **Transparent/ Opaque...** options.

SIZE AND POSITION

This lets you specify the **Size** of the frame and its **Position on Page**. **Margins** let you specify the amount of space between the outside edges of the frame and the text or picture inside it. A sample page box shows how your frame is sized and positioned on your page.

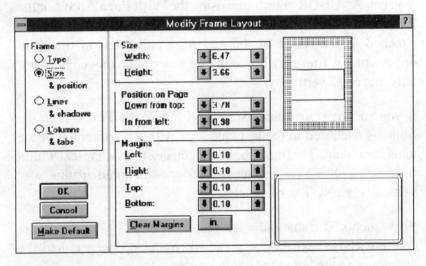

LINES AND SHADOWS

You can specify whether or not you want lines, the **Style** of lines and **Colour** and **Shadow** using this option. Within the **Shadow** box, the 4 arrows are used to indicate where the shadow has to be in relation to the Frame - bottom right, top right, bottom left or top left.

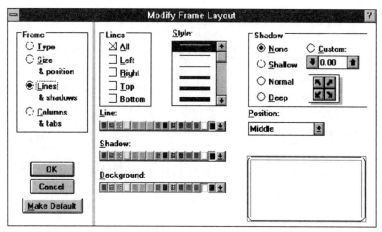

The **Position** box lets you specify the position of the lines relative to the margins of the frame.

Inside displays the lines ON the margins.
Close to Inside displays the lines just outside the margins.
Middle displays them halfway between the margins and the outside.
Close to Outside displays the lines just inside te edges of the frame.
Outside displays the lines on the outside edge of the frame.

COLUMNS AND TABS

This lets you specify the tabs and columns required within the frame.

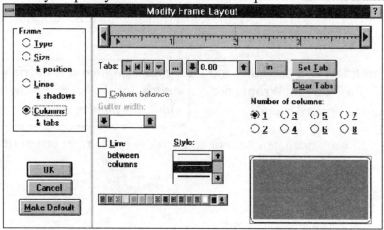

TIPS ON POSITIONING FRAMES

POSITIONING A FRAME WITHIN AN INDENTATION

> *This Frame is within the left indent from the margin*

If you've indented a paragraph or a number of paragraphs you can use Frames to insert notes into the indentation.

1   Create your Frame as above. Position it ABOVE the paragraphs that are indented.

2   **Select** your Frame.

3   Choose **Modify Frame Layout** from the **Frame** Menu (clicking the right mouse button when the frame is selected is the shortcut).

4   Select **No Wrap Around** from the **Text Wrap Around** options.

5   You might have to drag the frame into the required position.

TO WRAP DOCUMENT TEXT TO THE RIGHT OR LEFT OF A FRAME

You can position frames at the left or right margin to make text wrap around only one side of it.

This frame is at the right hand margin. The **Text Wrap** option is set to **Wrap Around**.

> *A Frame positioned at the right margin (could have been left) with text wrapping round it.*

If you want document text to appear only to the right or left of a frame this is how to do it.

122

TO FRAME EXISTING TEXT

1 Create a frame to the required size ABOVE the text you want to frame.

2 Specify **No Wrap Around** and **Transparent**.

3 Set any other options required and click **OK**.

4 Move and Size the Frame so that it surrounds the text.

IMPORT PICTURE

A fun feature to cheer up your documents or enhance your reports is the **Import Picture** option in the **File** menu.

There are 105 clip art images supplied with Ami Pro (they are AmiDraw graphic files with a .SDW extension). You can import these files directly into your Ami Pro documents.

Either create a frame the size you want and select it before importing a picture or just go ahead and import a picture to have it inserted automatically into a frame of the default size and specification.

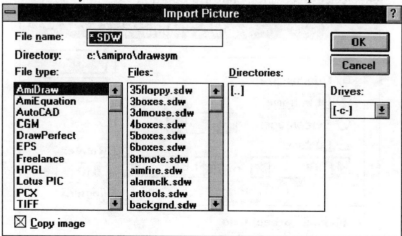

1 Choose **File, Import Picture**. The **Import Picture** dialogue box appears.

2 A list of the file types that can be imported directly into Ami Pro is shown in the **File Type** area.

3 Select the **File Type** and file required.

4 Leave the **Copy Image** box selected (this ensures a COPY of the file is inserted into the document and not the original) and click **OK**.

The chosen file is inserted into the selected frame in your document (if you didn't create and select a frame before importing a picture, a frame is automatically inserted using the default settings).

You can resize and rotate your picture by choosing **Frame, Graphics Scaling** and specifying the settings. The **Maintain Aspect Ratio** (when selected) keeps the picture in proportion and prevents distortion.

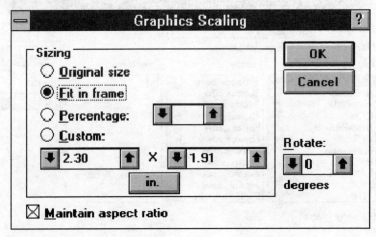

TO PASTE A PICTURE FROM ANOTHER WINDOWS APPLICATION

This is achieved by copy and paste between the applications.

1 Make the application that contains the picture the active window

2 Select the picture and copy it to the clipboard

3 Make the Ami Pro document you want the picture in the active window

4 Create a frame to the required size and select it (if you don't do this Ami Pro creates a frame automatically using the default settings).

5 Paste from the clipboard.

You can import a graphic file, paste a picture using the Windows clipboard or Paste link a picture from another Windows application that supports DDE or OLE (see Chapter 38).

Importing pictures is fun, but beware that pictures in an Ami Pro document take up a lot of disk space. You can cut down on the amount of disk space used by choosing **Tools, User Setup, Options** and setting the **Graphic Display Speed** options to **Conserve Disk Space** (this is the recommended setting if you've less than 10Mb available space).

If you've experienced tables before on a different Word Processing package, you'll know how useful they can be. Ami Pro's table feature is excellent!

You can use tables to   create parallel (side-by-side) columns
                                      input numeric data (like a mini spreadsheet)
                                      create data files for merge documents
                                      create forms
                                      and to chart from

CREATING A TABLE

Creating a table is simple. The first thing to decide is whether or not you want to create your table in the main document text or in a frame. A table created within the main document text is called a *page table*, a table created within a frame is called a *frame table*.

If your table is going to be bigger than a page you should create a page table. If it's less than a page and you want to be able to put it in a specific place, you should make it a frame table. (You simply select an empty frame of the correct size and location and create your table in it.)

1   Click the **Table** SmartIcon or choose **Tables** from the **Tools** menu.

2   The **Create Table** dialogue box appears.

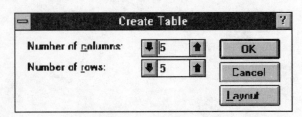

3 Specify the number of columns and rows you want in the table.

4 If you want to change the default layout for the table click the **Layout** button.

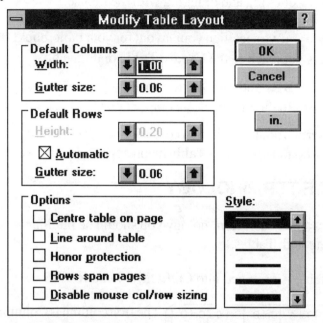

5 In the **Modify Table Layout** dialogue box you can specify the default width and gutter size for your columns; the default height and gutter size for your rows; the unit of measurement, (by clicking on the **Unit of Measurement** button until the unit you want is displayed); and you can select any **Options** required.

The **Options** let you:-

Centre table on page -sets it evenly between the left and right margins

Line around table - places a line around a PAGE TABLE

Honor protection - prevents Protected Cells being edited. This is a 2 stage process. Within a table you select any cells you want to protect, then set this option to make that protection effective.

Rows span pages - if set, allows data in a cell to continue onto to the next page without the whole row being taken down.

Disable mouse col/row sizing - prevents rows and columns being resized by clicking and dragging with the mouse.

6   Once you've specified your layout for your table, click **OK**. This takes you back to the **Create Table** dialogue box.

7   Click **OK** - and you are returned to your main document or frame. In the meantime an empty table has been inserted.

The insertion point is in the first cell, gridlines display the row, column and cell boundaries and a **Table** menu appears in the menu bar.

TABLE TERMINOLOGY

There's some basic terminology you should be familiar with when working with Tables.

Your table is arranged into COLUMNS and ROWS.

	Col A	Col B	Col C	Col D
Row 1				
Row 2		**Cell B2**		
Row 3				**Cell D3**

The first column is Column A, the next on is Column B, the next one is Column C and so on.

The first row is Row 1, the next on is Row 2, then Row 3, Row 4 and so on.

You can have up to 250 columns and 4000 rows in a Table!

Where a column and row intersect you get a CELL. The cell name, or address, is taken from the column and row that intersect to create it.

So we get cell A1, B2, D3, AA250, J3250 and so on.

KEYING TEXT AND NUMERIC DATA INTO A TABLE

Place the insertion point in the cell that you want to type the text or numeric data into, and simply type.

Text left aligns in a cell and if you've selected **Automatic Row Height** in the **Modify Table Layout** dialogue box, Ami Pro will automatically deepen a row to accommodate text that wraps in a cell.

MOVING AROUND IN A TABLE

■ To get into a Page Table click once anywhere within it. To get into a Frame Table double click anywhere within the table.

■ You can point and click to position the insertion point in the cell you want to be in.

■ To get out of a table simply click anywhere outside it.

When you're keying data into your table you might prefer to use the keyboard to move around it.

Useful keyboard options are:-

Tab and **Shift-Tab** to move forwards and backwards a CELL at a time.

Ctrl and ⇨ or ⊃o move you up or down a ROW at a time.

Ctrl and ⇨or   to move you left and right a COLUMN at a time.

Home and **End** to take you to the beginning or end of the current line within a CELL.

Home, Home to take you to the first column in the current row.

End, End to take you to the last column in the current row.

Ctrl-Shift-Tab to take you to the next tab position set within the current cell

SELECTION TECHNIQUES

To select:

> **the contents of a cell**, go to the cell and select the contents using any selection technique.
>
> **a number of cells** click and drag over the cells.
>
> **a rectangular range of cells**, click on the cell in one corner of the range to be selected, move to the cell in the corner diagonally opposite and **Shift-Click**.
>
> **a column**, move to the top of the column and click
>
> **a row**, move to the left of the row and click
>
> **the whole table**, choose **Select Entire Table** from the **Table** menu.

NB. For the above techniques, the insertion point must be within a Table. When you're in the right place for selecting a column or row the mouse pointer changes to a solid black arrow.

USING TABLES FOR SIDE-BY-SIDE COLUMNS

1   Set up your table with the number or rows and columns required (extra rows and columns can easily be added or deleted later).

2   Key the details into each cell as required - word-wrap happens automatically in cells provided the default **row height** in the **Modify Table Layout** dialogue box is set to **Automatic**.

ITEM	COMMENTS	PRICE
Victorian Dolls House	In excellent condition and bound to raise a lot of international interest. The asking price is modest.	£25,000 (minimum)
Toby Jugs	We've a lot of these at the moment - some in very good condition, others less so.	£15-£50

MODIFY COLUMN WIDTH

When you create a table, each column is of equal width, and the width depends on the number of columns and the length of typing line or the size of the frame.

To change the width of a column click and drag the vertical gridlines.

You can't widen columns if your table width overall is the full width of the typing line or frame.

USING A TABLE AS A MINI-SPREADSHEET

You can set up tabular work using tables and get Ami Pro to do automatic calculations on your data.

When keying in figures that are going to be used in calculations, ensure each figure is in its own cell and DON'T use currency symbols or commas - let the figures pick up the formatting in the **Table Text** paragraph style (if you don't like the style, modify it).

SALES FIGURES - 1st Quarter 1993

	JAN	FEB	MAR	TOTAL
A Smith	11,000	9,076	14,325	*34,401*
P Jones	9,500	10,243	12,467	*32,210*
B Peters	9,450	12,421	15,231	*37,102*
TOTAL	29,950	31,740	42,023	*103,713*

TABS WITHIN CELLS

There may be times when you need Tabs set up within a cell or group of cells to align your text and figures. You can do this simply by positioning the insertion point in the cell that you want to set tabs for (or select the cells if there's more than one) and set the tabs in the usual way - probably using the Ruler.

When you come to type your data in use **Ctrl-Shift-Tab** to move the insertion point to the tabs within the cells (**Tab** on its own will move the insertion point to the NEXT cell, and **Shift-Tab** moves the insertion point to the PREVIOUS cell).

CONNECTING CELLS

To connect cells, horizontally or vertically, for headings etc:

1   **Select** the cells to be connected

2   Choose **Connect Cells** from the **Table** Menu

TO TOTAL ROWS OR COLUMNS OF FIGURES

1   Position the insertion point in the cell that's to hold the Total

2   Choose **Quick Add** from the **Table** Menu and complete the dialogue box as required.

TO FORMAT THE CHARACTERS IN YOUR TABLE

Select the cells you want to format then apply the formatting you want - bold, italics, change font size and so on.

FORMULAE

You can add (**+**), subtract (**-**), multiply (*****), divide (**/**), calculate percentages (**%**) and total ranges using the sum function (**@sum(A1:A7)**).

You can build up quite complicated formulae to do your calculations and use parentheses ( ) to control the calculations.

To create or edit a formula:-

1 Put the insertion point in the cell you want to key the formula into

2 Choose **Edit Formula** from the **Table** menu

3 Key in or edit the formula

4 Click **OK**

Examples of formulae:-

> @sum(B7:B15)-C12
> A7+(B3*D6)-B1
> B7*15%
> (D10/D6)-C2

(For those of you familiar with spreadsheets, Lotus 1-2-3 syntax can be used for formulae and absolute addressing can be used to ensure the contents of a specific cell are always referenced regardless of where a formula is copied to).

Table Menu Options

The other options on the Table Menu allow for further enhancement and editing of your table. Here's a quick run through the options.

Lines & Colour... - You can put lines around a cell (or selected cells) by completing the dialogue box presented in this option.

Insert and Delete Column/Row ... - You can edit the number of columns and rows in your table by completing the dialogue boxes for these options.

Table	Window	Help
Modify Table Layout...		
Lines & Colour...		
Insert Column/Row...		
Delete Column/Row...		
Delete Entire Table		
Column/Row Size...		
Select Column		
Select Row		
Select Entire Table		
Connect Cells		
Headings		
Leaders		▶
Protect Cells		
Edit Formula...		
Quick Add		▶

Delete Entire Table -Use this to delete a table (the insertion point can be anywhere in the table). If you select the whole table and press the **Delete** key on your keyboard it's just the contents of the selected cells that get deleted, not the table itself.

Column/Row Size.... - You can use this option instead of dragging the gridlines if you prefer.

Select Column and **Select Row** - You can select the row or column your insertion point is in by choosing these options.

Select Entire Table - A quick way of selecting the whole Table.

Connect Cells - Used to connect selected cells - will connect cells horizontally and/or vertically.

Headings - If you choose this option when your insertion point is in a row, that row will be repeated as a heading at the top of each page the table runs to.

Leaders - Inserts a leader character before and after the cell content.

Protect Cells - Locks cells to prevent editing once **Honor Protection** is selected from the **Modify Table Layout** dialogue box.

Edit Formula - Allows you to create or edit formula in cells.

Quick Add - A quick way to insert the total of a column or row in a cell.

CREATING A DATA FILE IN A TABLE

If you want to use a Table to create a Data file for a merge operation (see Section 26), do this:

1 Set up a table in the normal way, with a COLUMN for each field and a ROW for each record (you can always add to these later if necessary).

   The table MUST start at the top of Page 1 in the document and there mustn't be any other text in the file.

2 In row 1 of your table type the field names - one in each cell.

3 Your first record goes in row 2. Move from cell to cell inserting the detail for each field.

Alternatively you can import the data into the cells in the table.

CREATING A FORM FROM A TABLE

1 Create your table in the normal way specifying the column and row details and options required.

2 Type in any LABELS your table has - for example headings, instructions and prompts.

3 Once you've done this for the whole form, select the cells that contain the labels and choose **Protect** from the **Table** menu.

4 Choose **Modify Table Layout** from the **Table** menu and select the **Honor Protection** checkbox.

You can't put the insertion point into cells that have been protected, so when you tab through the form, labels will be skipped and you can fill in the detail in the appropriate places.

TO PRINT ON A PRE-PRINTED FORM

If your form is based on a pre-printed one and you want to print out the variable information only into the pre-printed form, then this is how you do it.

1   Switch off the **Honor Protection** in the **Modify Table Layout** dialogue box.

2   Select the protected cells and choose **Mark Text** from the **Edit** menu.

3   Choose **Protected Text** from the list of options.

   (You might have to repeat those steps several times until all the Protected Cells are Marked).

4   Choose **Print** from the **File** Menu

5   Go into **Options** from the **Print** Menu

6   Select the **On Pre-printed Form** box and click **OK**

7   At the **Print** dialogue box click **OK** to start printing.

TO SAVE YOUR FORM

You can save your form as an Ami Pro document

OR

You can save the form as a Style Sheet, selecting **With contents**

■   It's usually best to save your form as a style sheet, then any time you want to complete a form, you simply select the form template when you create a new document. You'll then get a copy of the form in your new document ready for completion.

In Ami Pro you can sort entire documents, tables, or selected bits of your document or table.

The data you're sorting can be alphanumeric or numeric and can be sorted in ascending or descending order.

The data you're sorting will usually be in list format - set up using tabs or a table. Ami Pro recognises each row ending in a Carriage Return as a record, and the fields are separated from each other by a Tab character.

You can specify which word within the field the sort should be based on, and the delimiter (separator) between the fields if it's not a Tab.

If a record contains more than 1 paragraph you can specify this to ensure that the sort works properly.

You can perform multi-level sorts (up to 3 levels) so you could sort your customer list into alphabetical order, primarily by Region, within Region you could then have the Towns sorted alphabetically, and within the Town you could sort your customer names.

The easiest way to get the hang of the sort option is try it and see! You could type in the list below and try some sorting. It doesn't matter whether you use tabs or put it into a table, the sort works the same.

COMPANY	CONTACT	TELEPHONE NO
Russel Jones plc	Ann Anderson	071 333 1001
Tullis Gibson plc	Brian Gibson	031 445 2423
PC Perfection plc	John Butterworth	051 334 2255
Just Jumpers	Maureen McIntyre	0224 1432

Now, try sorting it into **Ascending** order by *Company* name to get the following result.

COMPANY	CONTACT	TELEPHONE NO
Just Jumpers	Maureen McIntyre	0224 1432
PC Perfection plc	John Butterworth	051 334 2255
Russel Jones plc	Ann Anderson	071 333 1001
Tullis Gibson plc	Brian Gibson	031 445 2423

1 First **select** the section to be sorted - exclude the titles.

2 Choose **Sort** from the **Tools** menu (if you haven't selected the data before doing this, Ami Pro prompts you with a dialogue box asking if you want to sort the entire text stream - respond as required and try again).

3 Under **Field**, all **Levels** should be set to 1, the **Type** should be set to **Alphanumeric** and the **Word** should be set to **1st**.

4 The **Sort Order** should be **Ascending** and the **Delimiter** is **Tab**.

5 The **No of paras in record** is 1 this time.

6 Click **OK**.

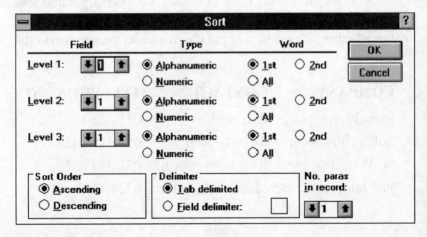

Try sorting the list in **Descending** order on *Contact* name.

COMPANY	CONTACT	TELEPHONE NO
Just Jumpers	Maureen McIntyre	0224 1432
Tullis Gibson plc	Brian Gibson	031 445 2423
PC Perfection plc	John Butterworth	051 334 2255
Russel Jones plc	Ann Anderson	071 333 1001

To get this, the dialogue box settings need to be:-

1 Under **Field, Level 1** should be set to **2** (it's the 2nd field in your record you're sorting on).

2 The **Type** is an **Alphanumeric** sort

3 Under **Word** select **2nd** (this will sort by Surname rather than Christian name)

4 Under **Sort Order** choose **Descending**.

Now try and get it into **Descending** order by *Company*

COMPANY	CONTACT	TELEPHONE NO
Tullis Gibson plc	Brian Gibson	031 445 2423
Russel Jones plc	Ann Anderson	071 333 1001
PC Perfection plc	John Butterworth	051 334 2255
Just Jumpers	Maureen McIntyre	0224 1432

The sorting examples above have sorted on one field only. If you want to sort on more than one field (up to 3) you do a Multi-Level sort.

You can key in the list below to experiment with a multi-level sort.

COMPANY	CONTACT	TEL NO	TOWN	REGION/ COUNTY
Just Jumpers	Maureen McIntyre	0224 1432	Aberdeen	Highland
Andrews Printing	John Andrews	041 445 5522	Glasgow	Strathclyde
Russel Electronics	Alison Johnstone	041 556 1132	Glasgow	Strathclyde
Fast Food Anywhere	Myra Brotherstone	031 556 7733	Dalkeith	Lothian
Original Designs	Jeffrey Lindsey	031 666 7722	Edinburgh	Lothian
Albert Jones plc	Tom Simpson	0553 113355	Gayton	Merseyside
PC Supplies	Jill Gardiner	0553 994455	King's Lynn	Norfolk
B Ready plc	Peter Ryan	041 556 1177	Glasgow	Strathclyde

Try sorting it into **Ascending** alphabetical Order by *Region*. The *Towns* in each region are to be sorted into **Ascending** order, and the *Companies* in each town are in **Ascending** order.

COMPANY	CONTACT	TEL NO	TOWN	REGION/ COUNTY
Just Jumpers	Maureen McIntyre	0224 1432	Aberdeen	Highland
Fast Food Anywhere	Myra Brotherstone	031 556 7733	Dalkeith	Lothian
Original Designs	Jeffrey Lindsey	031 666 7722	Edinburgh	Lothian
Albert Jones plc	Tom Simpson	0553 113355	Gayton	Merseyside
PC Supplies	Jill Gardiner	0553 994455	King's Lynn	Norfolk
Andrews Printing	John Andrews	041 445 5522	Glasgow	Strathclyde
B Ready plc	Peter Ryan	041 556 1177	Glasgow	Strathclyde
Russel Electronics	Alison Johnstone	041 556 1132	Glasgow	Strathclyde

To get this, the dialogue box **FIELD** settings should have:
> **Level 1** set to **5** (the main sort is on Region, Field 5, ascending order);
> **Level 2** set to **4** (within each region, you want the Town, Field 4, sorted into ascending order);
> **Level 3** set to **1** (within each town you want the Companies, Field 1, listed in ascending order).

Usually, the data you've to sort will be organised in rows as in the examples above, but you might find yourself wanting to sort data that's in paragraphs instead.

Let's say you had the information below to sort. Each record is arranged in 3 paragraphs (the empty line at the end of each record counts as 1 paragraph). The fields are separated by a comma (note that you don't put a comma after the last field in each paragraph, just press the **Enter** key).

Jones, Peter, 10:12:45
Joiner, London

Jackson, Amanda, 12:10:57
Sales Consultant, Manchester

Anderson, James, 14:06:53
Teacher, Birmingham

Dickson, Jennifer, 02:02:48
Secretary, Doncaster

Borthwick, Brian, 16:05:51
Driving Instructor, Keswick

Simpson, Sharon, 18:01:55
Marketing Manager, Manchester

Let's say we want to sort the records into alphabetical order on TOWN (field 5) and within town we want the records sorted on JOB TITLE (field 4)

1 In the **Sort** dialogue box, set **Level 1** to **5** (town), and **Level 2** to **4** (job title).

2 In the **Delimiter** options box select **Field Delimiter** and type a comma in the delimiter character box.

3 Set the **Number of Paragraphs** to 3 (each record consists of 3 paragraphs).

4 Click **OK**.

Your records should be in the order below - if not think about it and try again!!

Anderson, James, 14:06:53
Teacher, Birmingham

Dickson, Jennifer, 02:02:48
Secretary, Doncaster

Borthwick, Brian, 16:05:51
Driving Instructor, Keswick

Jones, Peter, 10:12:45
Joiner, London

Simpson, Sharon, 18:01:55
Marketing Manager, Manchester

Jackson, Amanda, 12:10:57
Sales Consultant, Manchester

You can use the Charting feature in Ami Pro to present your data graphically. Charts must be in a FRAME - you can either create the frame and select it before you create your chart, or you can let Ami Pro create your frame using the default frame settings.

Charts are produced from data YOU provide. You can either type your data into a Table or into your main document text, or you can key the data into the **Charting Data** dialogue box.

I think that the easiest way to create a chart in Ami Pro is from a Table. Let's go through the stages of charting the data below.

CREATING A CHART FROM EXISTING DATA

Key the data into a table (or set tabs for each column and key it in), then copy the whole thing to the clipboard.

	Jan	Feb	Mar	Apr	May	Jun	July	Aug	Sept	Oct	Nov	Dec
Rainfall (")	14	15	13	12	8	2	0	0	6	8	11	12
Hrs of Sun	3	4	6	7	9	10	10	10	8	6	4	2
Avg Temp	8	12	15	19	24	32	34	32	26	18	14	12

Click the **Charting** SmartIcon or choose **Charting** from the **Tools** menu. You're taken into the **Charting** dialogue box.

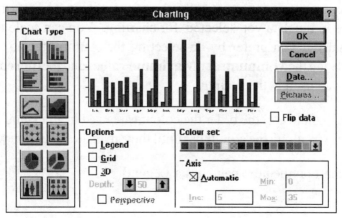

143

An example of your chart is displayed along with various options for manipulating and enhancing the presentation.

The information on the 1st row of the selected data is used to label the **X-axis** (the category axis). The information in the first column of the selected data can be used to produce a Legend for your chart by selecting the **Legend** box under **Options**. The rest of the data you selected is plotted in your chart.

You can change the type of chart by clicking the **Type** icon down the left of the **Charting** dialogue box.

You can change the way the data is plotted (from plotting rows of data to plotting columns of data) by selecting the **Flip Data** box.

You can produce a grid behind your chart by checking the **Grid** box under **Options**, and you can create a 3D effect by checking the **3D** box under **Options**.

If you opt for a 3D effect you can specify the depth of the 3D effect, and you can check the **Perspective** box to enhance the look of your 3D chart.

The axis are scaled automatically using the minimum and maximum values in the data you selected for charting. You can scale them manually if you prefer by de-selecting the **Automatic** box and specifying the **Minimum** and **Maximum** values and the **Increment** you want used in the scaling.

If you want to edit the order the colours are used in, click and drag the colours along the colour bar until they're in the order you want.

The chart on the next page has a **Legend**.

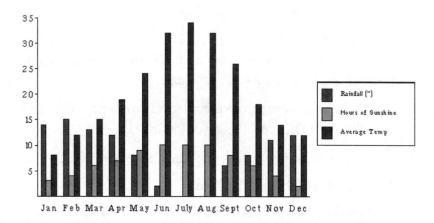

CREATING A CHART FROM DATA NOT IN YOUR DOCUMENT

There may be times when you want to produce a chart from data that doesn't exist in your document and you don't want to key it in, as it's just needed to produce the chart. If you choose **Charting** when there's no data in the clipboard for Ami Pro to chart you get the following message:-

If you want to enter the data directly into the **Charting Data** dialogue box, click **OK**.

The **Charting Data** dialogue box appears.

1 Complete it with the data for your chart - on the first row type in the X-Axis categories, in the first column type in data for the Legend, and key in the rest of the data.

2 Use your cursor keys to move from row to row - pressing **Enter** (which equals OK) only when you're finished.

3 Put a space between each item of data; ie in row 1 just type:

Jan[spacebar]**Feb**[spacebar]**Mar**

Ami Pro knows what you mean!

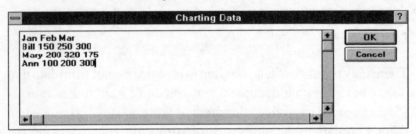

4 Once the data's in, click **OK** - or press **Enter**.

5 Complete the **Charting** dialogue box as required and click **OK**.

Your chart should appear in your document.

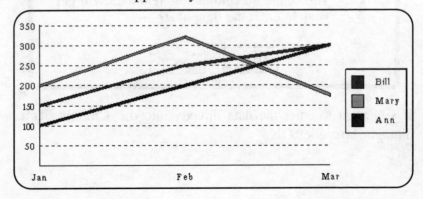

TO EDIT A CHART

To edit a chart that's already in your document:

1 Double click anywhere within the chart. This opens the **Chart Dialogue** box for the chart you double clicked in.

2 Edit the settings as required - if you want to edit the data click the **Data** button to take you through to the **Chart Data** dialogue box, make your changes and click **OK**.

3 When you've finished updating your chart, click **OK** in the **Chart Dialogue** box. The chart in your document will reflect the changes you've made.

TO DELETE A CHART FROM YOUR DOCUMENT

1 Click on the chart once to select it.

2 Press **Delete**.

You can enhance the appearance of your charts even further using the **Draw** feature, as you'll see in the next chapter.

The more artistic among you will have a lot of fun with this!

The less artistic (including me) will find it useful for producing things like organisation charts and enhancing Charts created using the **Charting** feature.

■ You MUST have a mouse to use this feature.

The more you experiment with this, the better you'll get, so just go for it!

A Drawing **must** be in a Frame so if you want to specify the size and style of frame your drawing is to be in, then do so. Next select the frame before choosing **Drawing**. If you choose **Drawing** without first creating a frame, Ami Pro automatically creates a frame using the options set in the **Create Frame** dialogue box.

Choose **Drawing** from the **Tools** menu or click the **Drawing** SmartIcon.

The drawing **Toolbar** appears and a **Draw** menu option appears on the Menu Bar.

The icons to the left (up to and including **[abc]**) are the **draw object icons**, the ones to the right are the **draw command icons**.

The best way to see what the icons do, is to try them and see.

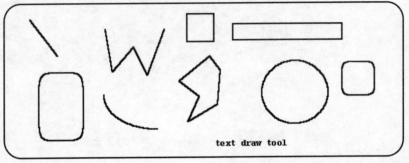

text draw tool

DRAWING AN OBJECT

The drawing tools start at the 3rd Icon from the left. They are straight line, polyline, polygon, rectangle, rectangle with rounded corners, ellipse, arc and text tool.

To select any tool, you click on it.

With the **line, rectangles, ellipse** and **arc,** you then move the mouse pointer to where you want to start drawing and click and drag to draw your shape. When you let go the button, the object is drawn.

If you want to draw a perfectly straight **horizontal** or **vertical line,** or **true circle** or **square** with either pointed or rounded corners, hold the **Shift** key down while you draw the shape.

With the **polyline** and **polygon:**

1 Point and click where you want the shape to start

2 Point and click at the position you want the line drawn to

3 Point and click at the next position and so on

4 Double click when you get to the last position to finish drawing the object.

With the **abc** (text) tool, point and click to position the insertion point where you want the text to appear in your drawing. Key in the required text, formatting as necessary.

SELECTING AN OBJECT

If you want to move or resize an object you must SELECT it first:

1 Choose the Pointer icon (the 1st one on the draw toolbar).

2 Point and click at the object you want to select.

3 Black handles appear on each corner and along each edge to show the edges of the object selected.

■ **To de-select an object**, click anywhere away from the object.

TO MOVE AN OBJECT

1 Select the object.

2 Then click anywhere within it, and drag to move it.

3 Let go the mouse button to drop the object in its new place.

If you want**to move a line**, click and drag while pointing anywhere along the line.

If you want **to leave one end of the line anchored**, but move the other end, hold the **Shift** key down while you click and drag the black handle at the end you want to move.

TO RESIZE AN OBJECT

1 Select the object.

2 Click and drag on any HANDLE on the outline. Drag in the direction necessary to make the object bigger or smaller.

Let's say that you wanted to create a simple organisation chart.

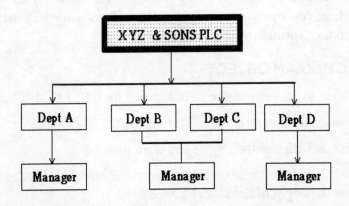

1 Draw the first rectangle to the desired size.

2 You can use copy and paste to create all of the other rectangles once you've got the first one. They paste on top of the original, so you then have to move them (drag) to the position they should be at.

3 To get the lines between the rectangles straight, hold the shift key down while you draw them.

FILL PATTERN

If you want shading or colour within a shape, choose the **Fill Pattern** icon (rightmost one). Choosing this icon displays the colour and fill pattern options.

If you want to change the fill and colour of an existing object:

1 Select the object you want to Fill.

2 Choose the **Fill Pattern** icon.

3 Choose the pattern or colour you want to fill the object with and click **OK**.

LINE STYLE

You can change the style, colour and endings to a line by choosing the **Line Style** icon (2nd last Icon). Choosing this icon displays the line style, colour and endings options.

If you want to modify an existing line:

1 Select the line you want to modify,

2 Choose the **Line Style** icon, complete the dialogue box as required and click **OK**.

Command Icons Summary

EXTRACT LINE & FILL

If you already have an object which has the line and fill options that you want to give to a new/another object, select the object and then choose the **Extract Line & Fill** icon (the 4th last one). This sets the **Line and Fill** dialogue box options to those of the selected object.

APPLY LINE AND FILL

If you already have an object in your drawing, and you want to apply the current line and fill options to it, select the object and choose the **Apply Line and Fill** Icon (3rd last one).

SELECTING MORE THAN ONE OBJECT AT A TIME

If you want to select more than one object from your drawing, select one object, then hold the **Shift** key down while you point and click at each additional object you want to select.

SELECTING ALL OBJECTS IN YOUR DRAWING

Choose the **Select All Icon** (the 1st draw command icon).

GROUPING OBJECTS

Once you've created your drawing from objects, you might want to group some (or all) of them into a single object. To do this, select the objects and then choose the **Group/Ungroup** icon (the 2nd draw command icon).

Grouped icons can easily be ungrouped again if you need to edit individual objects within the group. Simply select the object that has to be ungrouped and choose the icon again.

BRING TO FRONT or SEND TO BACK

If you've more than one object in the same location you can choose which object should be at the front or the back.

Select the object you want to Bring to Front or Send to Back. The **Bring to Front** icon is the 3rd draw command icon, the **Send to Back** is the 4th one.

ROTATE, FLIP HORIZONTALLY OR FLIP VERTICALLY

You can rotate or flip an object horizontally or vertically. Select the object to be rotated or flipped and choose the **Rotate** or appropriate **Flip** icon (5th to 7th draw command icons).

SHOW/HIDE GRID

It's often easier to align objects if the grid for the frame is displayed. You can use the **Show/Hide grid** icon to display or hide the grid when required (8th draw command icon).

SNAP TO

Aligns objects either automatically or manually to the grid specified for the frame (9th draw command icon).

HAND

The only other icon we've not discussed is the HAND. The Hand selects the whole picture so you can move it within the frame. You can use it to CROP the picture so that only part of it displays.

USING DRAW TO ENHANCE YOUR CHARTS

In the previous chapter we created charts to display your data graphically. Using the charting option you could produce a legend for your chart and put category details along the X-axis.

Most charts would, however, need a heading to explain what they were about - this is where **Draw** comes in.

	Spring	Summer	Autumn	Winter
Zoo	132,000	250,450	125,000	67,000
Botanics	750,324	450,025	578,021	365,024
City Farm	10,540	54,860	15,032	8,503

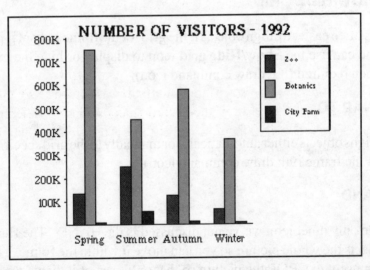

In your chart frame, you can choose draw and use any of the draw options to edit and enhance your chart. Each component of your chart is a separate object. You would use the text tool to add your headings.

The Merge feature can be used to produce personalised letters (your Reader's Digest and Time Share kind of thing!), labels and envelopes.

There are 3 stages to the Merge procedure:-

1 Create the DATA FILE

2 Create the MERGE DOCUMENT

3 Merge the two, to produce your final, personalised document

What is a DATA FILE?

A Data file can be a Name and Address list of customers, suppliers, personnel or indeed any file that contains information that you want to merge into a standard (merge) document.

The Data file is very structured. It contains the same kind of information on each individual or item within it.

All the Data relating to each individual or item is held in a RECORD. Each item of data within the record (name, address, telephone number, company) is held in a FIELD. Each field has a label, or NAME, that's used to identify it.

The first thing you must do before actually creating your Data file, is consider what information it is to hold and decide on your FIELD NAMES, to allow you to set up the structure of your Data File.

DATA FILE STRUCTURE

Record 1	*Field 1*	*Field 2*	*Field 3*	*Field 4*	*and so on*
Record 2	*Field 1*	*Field 2*	*Field 3*	*Field 4*	*and so on*
Record 3	*Field 1*	*Field 2*	*Field 3*	*Field 4*	*and so on*

What is a MERGE DOCUMENT?

Your Merge Document might be a letter, report, envelope, label - any kind of document you want to Merge the details from your Data File into.

The Merge Document contains the standard text (if any) for your final document, the field names from the data file that contains the details you want to merge in, and any formatting (margins, line spacing) that the final document will have.

What happens during the MERGE procedure?

When you Merge your Data File and your Merge Document, the field names in the Merge Document are replaced with the detail from the Data File.

The result is a personalised document, containing standard text from the Merge Document (*if* it had standard text - labels and envelopes usually don't have), and the detail read from each record in the Data File.

Let's try it and see how it works.

STARTING THE MERGE PROCEDURE

1 Choose **Merge ...** from the **File** Menu

2 The **Welcome to Merge** dialogue box appears.

3 Select stage **1** to **create a data file** and click **OK**.

4 The **Select Merge Data File** dialogue box appears. As you've not created a data file yet select **New...** (if you'd already one set up, you could choose the name of the data file you want to use and select **Edit ...** to edit it, or just specify the drive, directory and name to select it as Stage 1 of the merge process).

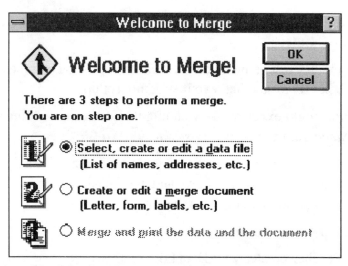

5 The **Create Data File** dialogue box appears.

This is where you create the STRUCTURE for your data file - you specify the FIELD NAMES.

Field Names and Records are separated from each other by characters called DELIMITERS. The default Field delimiter is ~ and the default Record delimiter is I. If you don't want the standard delimiters, choose **Options** and select from the list provided.

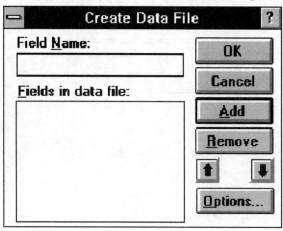

6 Key in the first field name for your Data file and click **Add** or press **Enter**.

7 Enter the rest of the field names until your list is complete, then click **OK** to say that's your structure set up.

You could experiment by adding the following field names:-
Name, Address, Town, Postcode, Tel No.

8 If you want to rearrange the order of field names, select the field name that you want to move and use the navigation buttons to move the field up or down the list.

9 Click **OK** when you're finished.

Ami Pro then creates your Data File.

The first row of the Data File lists the Delimiters ie ~ | The second row lists the field names with the field delimiter after each one, and the record delimiter at the end of the record.

The **Data File entry** screen is then displayed (it looks like an index card) to allow you to key in the detail to each record.

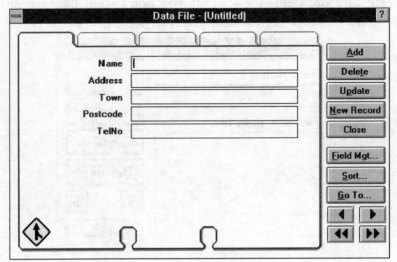

ADDING RECORDS

1   Key the detail into each field, pressing **Enter** after each.

2   When the record is complete click **Add**.

■ **You can edit and manipulate your data file from this screen.**

MOVING BETWEEN RECORDS

You can move between the records in your Data File using the forward or backward buttons - they take you through your Data File one record at a time. The fast forward and fast backward buttons take you to the last or first record in your datafile. You can use the **Go To...** button to specify which record you want to Go To.

DELETING RECORDS

Once a Record is displayed, you can delete it with the **Delete** button.

UPDATE RECORD

Once a record is displayed, you can edit the record and choose the **Update** button to store the new data.

NEW RECORD

If you want to add another record, click the **New Record** button and an empty record is presented for you to complete.

EDIT THE STRUCTURE OF YOUR DATA FILE

To edit the STRUCTURE of your data file, choose **File Mgt ...** You are presented with a dialogue box that lets you Insert and Rename fields.

To **INSERT** a field name:

1 Move down the list of field names until you're at the place you want the new field to be.

2 Type in the new field name and choose **Insert**.

3 Complete the dialogue box to indicate where you want the new field name put.

To **RENAME** a field:

1 Move onto the field name you want to rename

2 Type in the new name you want that field to have and choose **Rename**.

SORT DATA FILE

Your records appear in your Data File in the order that you keyed them in. If you want them in a particular order choose **Sort** and complete the dialogue box as required.

CLOSING AND SAVING

Once you've completed your Data File, choose **Close**.

You're asked whether or not you want to save your Data File - choose **Yes** and specify the drive, directory and filename you want it to have.

You're then ready to move on to Stage 2 of the merge process - creating your Merge Document.

CREATING THE MERGE DOCUMENT

Key in your merge document text (if any).

When you want to insert a field name from your data file, select the field name from the list in the **Insert Merge Field** box and click **Insert**. When your merge document is complete, click **Continue Merge** from the **Insert Merge Field** box.

MERGE & PRINT

Select stage 3 from the **Welcome to Merge** dialogue box. The **Merge** dialogue box appears.

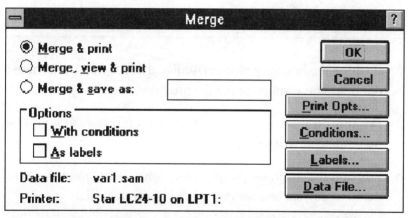

You can choose whether you want to **Merge & print**, **Merge, view and print** or **Merge and save as** a File (you have to give a name for your result document if you choose this option).

If you select the **Print Opts...** button you go to the **Print** dialogue box where you can specify the print options required.

Choose **OK** to merge all the records in the current Data File with the Merge Document.

MERGE CONDITIONS

If you want to do a selective merge (you don't want ALL your records merged but only ones that meet certain criteria) choose the **Conditions ...** button.

The **Merge Conditions** dialogue box appears.

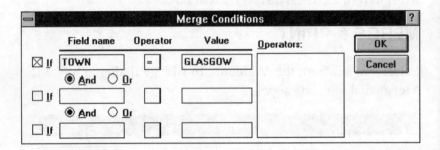

1   Position the insertion point in the **Field name** field, and choose the field you want from the list provided.

2   Position the insertion point in the **Operator** field, and choose the operator you want

3   Position the insertion point in the **Value** field, and key in the detail to be checked for in the field in the data file.

You can specify up to 3 conditions.

■   If you choose **AND** between conditions, a match is only made when all conditions are met.

■   If you choose **OR** between conditions, a match is made if either or any of the conditions are met.

For example, you could set 2 conditions

NAME = *Anderson*, **AND** TOWN = *Edinburgh*.

This would only select records where BOTH conditions were met - ie the *Anderson*'s in *Edinburgh*.

If you set 2 conditions

NAME = *Anderson* **OR** TOWN = *Edinburgh*,

This would select all the records where *Anderson* was in the Name field AND all the records where the Town field had *Edinburgh* in it. So you would get Anderson's in London, Manchester, Leeds, and Jones', Borthwick's, McDonald's from Edinburgh.

4 Click **OK** when you've set up your conditions.

When you return to the **Merge** dialogue box the **Options, With conditions** checkbox is selected. If at some stage you want to do a merge using the whole data file, but don't want to cancel the conditions in the **Merge Conditions** dialogue box, simply de-select the checkbox.

5 Click **OK** when your options are all set.

LABELS

If you choose the **Labels...** button from the Merge dialogue box you're given the **Merge Labels** dialogue box so you can specify your label layout (more on this in the next chapter).

If you choose the **Data File...** button you're given the **Select Data File** dialogue box so that you can select a different Data File if necessary.

USING A TABLE AS YOUR DATAFILE

If you prefer, you can set up a table and key your Data File details into it.

Your Table MUST be on the 1st page of your document and there can be no other text in your file.

1　Create a Table with a COLUMN for each field and a ROW for each record.

2　In the first row type a field name at the top of each column

3　Add the detail for each record in the rows of the Table.

4　Save your file and close it.

5　When you choose **File, Merge** you can select this file as your Data File for the Merge.

You can use any Table editing techniques to manipulate your data - if you need more fields, you can add more columns; if you need more records you can add more rows; you can sort your table to get the records into the order you want.

If you want to DELETE a field from the structure of your Data File, you can do so in a Table by deleting a column - you can't do it in a Merge Data File!!

In addition to using Merge for personalised letters or forms as in the previous chapter, it's easy to use your Data Files to prepare and print labels or envelopes.

1 Choose **File, Merge** and at Stage 1 of the Merge process select the Data File you want to create your labels or envelopes from.

FOR LABELS

2 At Stage 2 of the Merge process, create a New merge document using the **_LABEL.STY** style sheet.

This style sheet contains layouts for the Avery laser labels.

3 Select the label you want to use from the list provided.

4 Choose **Merge** (select **Manual** if you want to type the detail for your label through the keyboard, select **Custom** if you want to set up your own label specification).

5 Insert the Field Names from your Data File where you want them merged into your label.

6 Select **Continue Merge...** when your label is set up.

7 Choose Stage **3** from the **Welcome to Merge** dialogue box.

8 In the **Merge** dialogue box choose **Labels...** and edit the number across and down, label indents and number of times you want each label printed as necessary. Click **OK.**

9 Under **Options** in the **Merge** dialogue box select the **As Labels** option.

10 Click **OK.**

FOR ENVELOPES

1 At Stage 2 of the Merge process, create a New merge document using the **_ENVELOP.STY** style sheet.

2 Complete or edit the **Default Information** dialogue box and the **Optional Information** dialogue box as required (if you don't want to insert or edit anything as they're presented just click **OK**).

3 Complete your Envelope document with the field names required from your Data File.

4 Choose **Continue Merge....**

5 Choose Stage **3** at the **Welcome to Merge** dialogue box.

6 Complete the **Merge** dialogue box as required.

7 Click **OK**.

- 6 -
Working with Longer Documents

All of the features we've discussed so far are useful in Multi-page documents. However, there are some features that are especially useful - like Widow & Orphan protect, headers and footers, automatic page numbering and controlling automatic page breaks. That's the kind of thing we're looking at in this chapter.

WIDOW & ORPHAN PROTECT

With widow & orphan protect switched on, you prevent the first line of a paragraph being left behind as the last line on a page, and the last line of a paragraph falling over to be the first line on a page - either situation being considered undesirable.

Select the **Widow & Orphan** checkbox in **Tools, User SetUp, Options ...** (if it isn't already selected), to activate this protection.

HEADERS & FOOTERS

A *Header* is text that you want to appear in the top margin of each page, a *Footer* is text in the bottom margin of each page. There are 2 kinds of Header and Footer in Ami Pro - FIXED or FLOATING.

With FIXED headers and footers, the same header or footer appears in the top or bottom margin of every page.

To create a fixed header or footer:

1   Point and click in the top or bottom margin of your page

2   Type in the desired header or footer, then point and click back in the main text area and continue work. The header and footer will appear on EVERY page of your document.

Note:- you must be in **Layout Mode**, and it's easier to see the top and bottom margins if you've selected the **Margins In Colour** checkbox in the **View Preferences** dialogue box.

If you don't want the same header or footer on every page, you must use Floating Headers or Footers.

With FLOATING headers and footers, you put a marker in the text you want the header or footer attached to and type the header or footer in the top or bottom margin.

To insert a floating header or footer:

1 Place the insertion point in the text you want the header or footer to be attached to.

■ If you want the header or footer to start on the current page, the insertion point must be on the first line of that page. If your insertion point is not on the first line of the page, the header or footer will start on the next page.

2 Choose **Page, Header/Footer...** and click **Floating Header/ Footer...**

3 The **Floating Header/Footer** dialogue box appears.

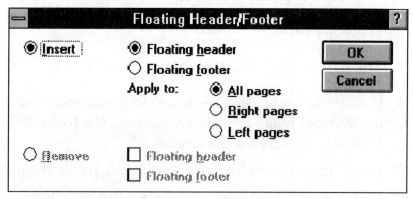

4 Complete it as necessary to indicate whether the Header or Footer is required on **All** pages, **Right** pages or **Left** pages.

5   Click **OK** when you're finished.

■   The insertion point will be placed in the Top or Bottom margin of the page where the header or footer will start.

6   Type in the desired text and return to the main document text area by clicking in it with the mouse or pressing **Esc**.

You can view floating header/footer marks by selecting the **Marks** checkbox in the **View Preferences** dialogue box.

As you edit your document, if the text with the floating header/footer mark should move to another page, then the header or footer will "float" with it.

The header or footer will appear on the pages specified until another header/footer instruction is encountered.

If you want to STOP displaying your floating headers or footers for part of your document, go through the procedure for setting up a floating header or footer, but don't key any text in to the margin area. This "empty" header or footer will have the effect of switching the header or footer off.

TO REMOVE A FLOATING HEADER OR FOOTER

1   Go to the floating header or footer mark for the particular header or footer you want to remove (you can use **Go To** for this). Place the insertion point ON the mark.

2   Choose **Page, Header/Footer...** then **Floating Header/Footer**

3   Choose **Remove** and select the Floating Header or Floating Footer checkbox as required.

4   Click **OK**.

PAGE NUMBERING

1 Place the Insertion point in the top or bottom margin where you want the page numbering to start.

2 Choose **Page, Page Numbering**

The **Page Numbering** dialogue box appears.

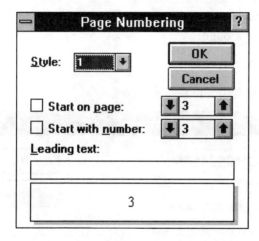

3 Select the style of numbering required. Specify the page to start numbering on, and which number to start with. If you want to have any leading text, eg "Page" in front of your number, key the text in the **Leading text** field.

4 The lower box displays a sample of how your selected page numbering set up will look.

5 Click **OK**.

REMOVE PAGE NUMBERING

If you want to remove your page numbering, select the page numbering on any page of your document and press **Delete.**

PAGE BREAKS

Ami Pro gives automatic page breaks when it gets to the end of a page, so normally you don't need to worry about them.

Sometimes however you'll want to specify where a Page Break occurs.

If you've reached a point where you want a page break, but it's not at the bottom of a page:

1 Choose **Page, Breaks...**

2 The **Breaks** dialogue box appears.

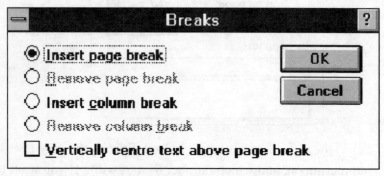

3 Complete as required and click **OK**.

You can view page breaks by selecting the **Marks** checkbox in the **View Preferences** dialogue box.

TO REMOVE A MANUAL PAGE BREAK

1 Go to the **Page Break** mark.

2 Position the insertion point ON the mark.

3 Choose **Page, Breaks...** and **Remove page break**.

When working with any document, but perhaps particularly so when working with long documents, the GoTo, Find & Replace and Bookmark features can be very useful. Let's look at the Go To first.

GO TO

To access the **Go To** dialogue box click the **Page Status** indicator on the status bar, or choose **Edit, Go To**. (The keyboard shortcut is **Ctrl-G**).

The **Go To** dialogue box appears.

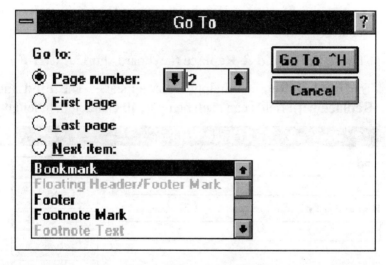

You can use Go To to go to a page number, the first page or last page in a document. Using any of these options positions the insertion point at the beginning of the specified page.

You can also tell Ami Pro to Go To a Bookmark, Floating Header/ Footer Mark, Footer, Footnote Mark or Footnote Text. When you select any of these items, the **Next Item** option becomes selected.

29 Go To, Find and Bookmarks

Once you've specified what you want to "Go To", click the **Go To ^H** button to move the insertion point within your document. If you've chosen to Go To a *next item*, you can move onto the next occurrence of the same item by using **^H** when the insertion point is within your text.

FIND & REPLACE

You can use the Find & Replace feature to either Find text or Find & Replace text.

1 Position the insertion point where you want to start your Find & Replace.

2 Choose **Edit, Find & Replace** (keyboard shortcut **Ctrl-F**).

The **Find & Replace** dialogue box appears. The **Find** and **Replace with** fields can each be up to 40 characters in length.

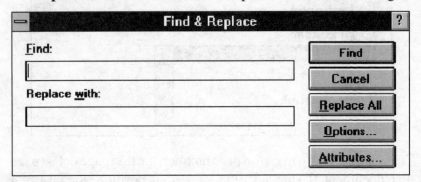

FIND

If you just want to Find text, key the text into the **Find** field and click **Find**. The Find will stop the first time it finds what you've requested and presents the **Find & Replace** dialogue box.

Complete the dialogue box as required.

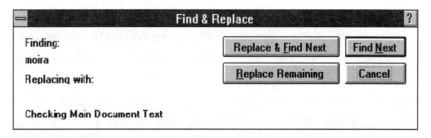

SELECTIVE FIND & REPLACE

If you want to do a *selective* **Find & Replace** - you don't want every occurrence of the Find text replaced - complete both the **Find** and the **Replace with** field in the dialogue box and click **Find**.

You can then specify when to make the replacement as each occurrence of the Find text is found, in the **Find & Replace** dialogue box.

GLOBAL FIND & REPLACE

If you want to do a Global replacement - that is change every occurrence of the Find text to the Replace with text - choose **Replace All** in the **Find & Replace** dialogue box.

OPTIONS

From the **Find & Replace** dialogue box, you can choose **Options** to give additional instructions - **Find** options, **Replace** options, **Range and Direction** options and **Find & Replace Type** can be specified.

You can also select the **Attributes** button from the **Find & Replace** dialogue box, and give specific information relating to the character formatting of the find and/or replace string.

29 Go To, Find and Bookmarks

■ Find & Replace can be very useful to correct wrong information - throughout your report you've mentioned Dr D MacIver, only to discover it was really Mr D MacIntyre - Find & Replace can fix this in no time.

Another time to use it is when you find you've to type in a technical term or foreign name, that really slows you down, or if you've a long company name to type repeatedly throughout your file, eg *British Isles Widows and Orphans plc*. You can key in an abbreviation or code where the term or phrase should be, eg BIWO or !?! and then do a Find and Replace to change your code to the real thing! (Make sure your code is unique though!!).

BOOKMARKS

You can use the Bookmark feature to insert a mark into your document at an important point - in text, a table, a frame, a header or footer - and then use Go To to move through your document to the place of the bookmark. (Handy when you know you've to check something out and then get back to a certain point of your document to input or edit information).

You can either place the insertion point where you want the Bookmark to go or select the table, frame, text, header or footer you want it attached to.

1 Choose **Bookmark** from the **Edit** menu. The **Bookmark** dialogue box appears.

If there are already Bookmarks in your document, they are listed in the **Current bookmark** list.

2 Give your Bookmark a name (up to 17 characters, alpha or alphanumeric - the name can't start with a number or be all numbers).

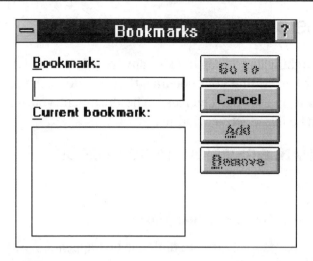

3 Click **Add**.

The Bookmark is inserted into your document - it won't be visible on the screen and it won't print.

To GO TO the next Bookmark choose **Bookmark** from the **Next item** list in the **Go To** dialogue box and click **Go To**.

To GO TO a specific Bookmark, choose **Edit, Bookmark...** then choose the one required from the **Current list** and click **Go To**.

To remove a Bookmark choose the Bookmark from the **Current list** and click **Remove**.

REVISION MARKING

You might want to keep track of any insertions and deletions you make when editing your document. If you do, then use Revision Marks to mark your changes. The document you want to edit should be in the active window.

TO ENABLE REVISION MARKING MODE

Either:

1 Choose **Tools, Revision Marking....**

The **Revision Marking** dialogue box appears.

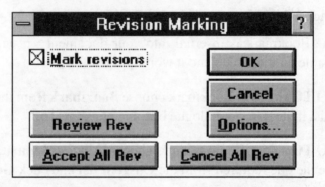

2 Select the **Mark revisions** checkbox to switch the function on.

Or

1 Click the **Typing Mode** button on the Status Bar until it says **Rev**

REVISION MARKING OPTIONS

You can customise HOW you want your revisions to appear on the screen.

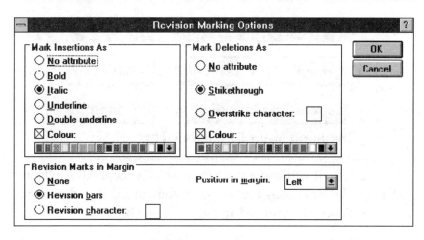

From the **Revision Marking** dialogue box, choose **Options** to specify:-

■ The appearance of your insertions and deletions in your document

■ The revision mark indicator to use (if any)

■ The position of the revision mark indicator if you're using one (Left, Right or Left & Right margins)

With Revision Marking enabled, any insertions and deletions you make will appear as specified in the Revision Marking options.

REVIEW REVISIONS

Once your editing is complete you can choose **Review** from the **Tools, Revision Marking** dialogue box to review each revision mark in turn.

The **Review Revision Marking** dialogue box appears when each insertion or deletion is found. Complete the dialogue box as required and continue.

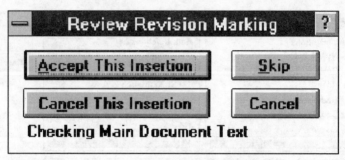

Alternatively, if you know that you want to **Accept All Revisions** or **Cancel All Revisions** you've made, you can choose either option from the **Tools, Revision Marking** dialogue box.

DOCUMENT COMPARE

Along the same lines as Revision Marking you have a Document Compare feature.

This feature lets you compare the CURRENT document, with another document on disk. It's a very useful feature when you've edited a document, and then decide you want to see what changes you've actually made, compared with the original.

TO COMPARE DOCUMENTS

The current document should be in the active window - this will probably be your most recent version of a file or a newly edited file (this gets called your SOURCE file).

1 Choose **Tools, Doc Compare...**

2 In the **Doc Compare** dialogue box, indicate the file you want your document to be compared with (this is your COMPARED file) - probably the previous version of the same document, or a similar document.

3 Click **OK**

THE RESULTS FROM A DOCUMENT COMPARE

Once the documents have been compared, Ami Pro displays the differences between the 2 documents as marked revisions in the SOURCE file.

Anything found in the SOURCE file that isn't in the COMPARED file is marked as an **Insertion**.

Anything found in the COMPARED file that isn't in the SOURCE file is marked as a **Deletion**.

The COMPARED file isn't changed in any way.

You can then use the **Tools, Revision Marking...** feature to review each revision and accept or cancel it as required.

Footnotes can be inserted into your main document text or into a Table. The text associated with a footnote appears at the bottom of the page the footnote mark is on, or under the Table if used in the table environment.

ADD A FOOTNOTE

1   Position the insertion point where you want your Footnote marker and choose **Tools, Footnotes...**

The **Footnotes** dialogue box appears.

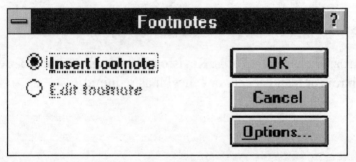

2   Simply click **OK** to insert your footnote marker.

3   Type the text you want in the footnote area.

4   Press **Esc** or point and click with the mouse to return the insertion point to the main document text area.

FOOTNOTE OPTIONS

If you want to modify the footnote settings choose **Options** from the **Footnotes** dialogue box.

If you want Endnotes (appear at the end of the document) rather than Footnotes (appear at the bottom of the page the footnote mark is on) select the **Make endnotes** checkbox.

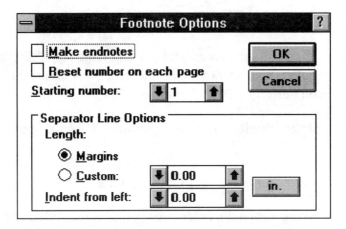

If you want your footnotes numbering reset on each page select the **Reset number on each page** and specify the number the footnote numbering is to start at.

You can specify the length and position of the line separator (the line that separates the main body text from the footnote area) in the **Separator Line Options** area.

EDITING FOOTNOTE TEXT

In **Layout** mode, click in the footnote area and edit the text as necessary

OR

Place the insertion point on the Footnote number and choose **Tools, Footnotes... Edit Footnote**.

REMOVING A FOOTNOTE

Select the footnote number in the main document area and press **Delete**.

MODIFY THE STYLE OF A FOOTNOTE

If you want to use a different kind of numbering sequence, or use letters or bullets instead for your footnote, or if you want it in italics or bold you must modify the footnote STYLE.

Choose **Style, Modify Style** and select the **Footnote** paragraph style.

Edit as required and save your modified style.

When working with a document that contains footnotes, Ami Pro keeps your footnote numbering sequence correct regardless of the editing you do. So, if you move or delete text that contains a footnote mark, or if you insert or delete footnote marks, Ami Pro will automatically renumber as necessary.

Outlining is a very useful technique to use when organising a long, STRUCTURED document - a report, minutes or a manual. If you use Outline Mode to view your document, you can see and modify the STRUCTURE of your document as well as the content.

Ami Pro provides 9 levels of outline. Each level has a paragraph style assigned to it - so you should be familiar with styles if you hope to get the most out of outlining! You can use the paragraph styles available in the current document or you can use the paragraph styles provided in **_OUTLINE.STY** - it's up to you.

There are 4 steps to creating an outline:-

1   Assign an Outline level to your paragraph styles

2   Access Outline Mode

3   Key in your document, with your headings at the desired level

4   Print your Outline document

Outline Mode and Layout Mode

Text editing within Outline Mode is the same as in Layout Mode.

Where it differs is in the way you can set up and manipulate the STRUCTURE of your document. You can PROMOTE or DEMOTE paragraphs, with or without subordinate text. You can COLLAPSE or EXPAND outline levels to show the structure of your document in the desired detail, and you can MOVE levels with or without subordinate levels.

Some new terminology you should become accustomed to:-

LEVELS   1-9 (used to structure your document) or None

PROMOTE   Takes a level higher eg level 3 up to level 2

DEMOTE   Takes a level lower eg level 3 down to level 4

SUBORDINATE Lower levels are subordinate to higher levels eg level 3 is subordinate to level 2

COLLAPSE   Hide subordinate levels

EXPAND   Show subordinate levels

Let's see how it works.

STEP 1 - ASSIGN PARAGRAPH STYLES TO EACH LEVEL OF OUTLINE

1 Choose **Outline Styles** from the **Style** Menu. The **Outline Styles** dialogue box opens.

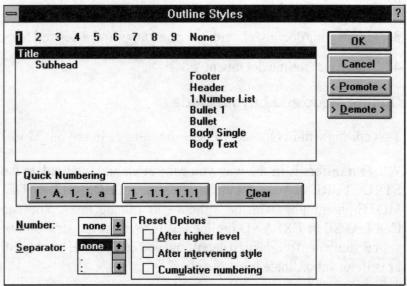

2 Select the style you want to promote or demote and click the **Promote** or **Demote** button until it is at the level required (or you can drag the selected style to the level you want.)

In the example above the TITLE paragraph style is at level 1, the SUBHEAD paragraph style is at level 2 and the others have no paragraph style assigned to them.

3 Click **OK**

_OUTLINE.STY

If you want, you can use the paragraph styles in _OUTLINE.STY. To use these paragraph styles in your outline:-

1 Go into Outline Mode (Choose **View, Outline Mode**)

2 Choose **Outline, Use Outline Styles**

Ami Pro now uses the formatting information in _OUTLINE.STY. To go back to the formatting in your document choose **Outline, Use Outline Styles** again.

STEP 2 - ACCESS OUTLINE MODE

Choose **Outline Mode** from the **View** Menu

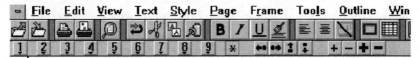

The **Outline Mode** icons appear, and **Outline** appears in the Menu Bar.

The Outline Icons fall into 2 categories:-

Outline Level icons (1-9 and *). You use these icons to specify the number of levels you want to view in your outline - selecting 3 would display only levels 1, 2 and 3 for the whole document; selecting the * would display levels 1-9 and any text that has no level assigned to it, eg body text; selecting level 1 would only display your level 1 headings. You can use these icons to view the structure of your whole document to the level required.

Outline Command icons. From left to right these icons are used to promote levels; demote levels; move levels up or down; expand and collapse to next level only; expand and collapse all levels.

You'll also find options in the **Outline** Menu that let you do the same things.

STEP 3 - KEY IN YOUR DOCUMENT, WITH YOUR PARAGRAPHS AT THE DESIRED LEVEL

Now you can key in your document.

PROMOTE and DEMOTE

Use the promote/demote icons to move your paragraphs to the correct level. If you've keyed in a paragraph at the wrong level, either select the paragraph or put the insertion point anywhere within the paragraph, and click the **Promote** or **Demote** button until you've got it at the correct level.

Notice that once you're at a level, pressing **Enter** keeps you at the same level. If you want the next paragraph promoted or demoted, use the appropriate icon once you've pressed **Enter**.

MOVE UP OR DOWN

If you need to MOVE a paragraph, either select the paragraph(s) or put the insertion point within the paragraph to be moved and click the move up or move down icons as necessary.

COLLAPSE AND EXPAND

The plus and minus icons expand and collapse parts of your outline.

The *small* plus and minus icons expand and collapse the subordinate text for the paragraph the insertion point is in, ONE LEVEL AT A TIME.

The *big* plus and minus icons expand and collapse ALL the subordinate text for the paragraph the insertion point is in.

You can use these to display specific areas of your outline to the desired level.

OUTLINE BUTTONS

These appear down the left hand side of your Outline (if there's nothing there, go into **View, View Preferences**, select **Outline Buttons** and click **OK**).

PLUS BUTTON Indicates the paragraph is using a paragraph style set to level 1-9 and that it has subordinate text.

MINUS BUTTON Indicates the paragraph is using a paragraph style set to level 1-9 and that it has no subordinate text.

FILLED IN PLUS BUTTON Indicates the paragraph is using a paragraph style set to level 1-9 and that it has subordinate text that has been collapsed or hidden.

BOX BUTTON The paragraph is using a paragraph style set to an outline level of none.

NOTE: You can use the **Plus** buttons to expand and contract subordinate text. Simply double click on the **Plus** button.

You can also click and drag the **Plus** buttons to move text to a different location.

STEP 4 - PRINT YOUR OUTLINE DOCUMENT

In Outline Mode, display your document to show the level of detail you want to print.

Print your document in the normal way.

NUMBERING YOUR OUTLINE

You'll probably find that there are times when you want to number all or part of your outline. This is easily done using **Style, Outline Styles**.

There are 2 quick numbering options pre-set for use. You can select either of these styles by simply clicking the button.

Alternatively, you can set up you own customised numbering setup. To do this:-

1   Select the heading level you want to number

2   Choose the Number style you want from the **Number** list.

3   If you want a separator between you number and text, choose the one you want from the separator list.

RESET OPTIONS

These options allow you to reset your numbering at specific times.

After Higher Level

The numbering restarts after the Outline has reached a paragraph at a higher level.

After an Intervening Style

The numbering restarts after the Outline reaches a paragraph style set to another outline level or none.

Cumulative Numbering

Ami Pro automatically incorporates the numbers specified in paragraph styles set to a higher level into paragraph numbers set for the lower levels to give 1, 1.1, 1.1.1, 1.1.1.1., etc

The Outline below has been numbered using the **Quick Numbering** Option 1.

I.　　　COMPUTER BOOKS

A. Word Processing

1. Beginner/Intermediate

i. Get Going With Ami Pro 3

An introductory book to get the nervous user started. Takes you through the basics so you can create, edit and print your documents confidently.

ii. Get Going With Wordperfect for Windows

A beginners book for the Windows version of this popular DOS package.

2. Advanced

i. Tricks and Tips for Ami Pro

ii. Tricks and Tips for Wordperfect for Windows

32 Outline Modes & Numbering

B. Spreadsheets

1. Beginner/Intermediate

i. Starting with Supercalc

2. Advanced

i. Tricks and Tips for Supercalc

ii. Tricks and Tips for Excel

C. Databases

1. Beginner/Intermediate

i. Getting Started with DBASE

ii. Dataease for Beginners

2. Advanced

i. Moving on with Dataease

II.   LANGUAGE BOOKS

A. French

1. Conversational

i. Get by in French

2. Business

i. Business correspondence in French

OUTLINE STYLE SHEETS

There are 3 Outline Style Sheets (in addition to _outline.sty used in Outline mode) _outlin1.sty, _outlin2.sty and _outlin3.sty which you may want to look at.

They have different PAGE layouts and PARAGRAPH styles which you might find suit your needs.

To use them, simply base your new document on the Style Sheet required and continue as above.

Another useful feature for those of you with long documents is the Table of Contents (TOC) generator. Your TOC can have up to 9 levels of indentation, and can be generated within the document to which it applies, or to a separate file.

There are 2 stages to producing a TOC.

■ FIRST, you have to specify WHAT has to go into your TOC.

This can be done by using heading paragraph styles to format your headings. If you use this method each style you're using for the headings must be assigned a level from 1-9.

OR

You can select the text from your document and mark it as a TOC entry.

■ SECOND, you have to generate the Table of Contents.

Let's look at the 2 ways in which you can specify WHAT has to go into your Table of Contents.

TO ASSIGN TOC LEVELS TO PARAGRAPH STYLES

1 Choose **Tools, TOC Index...**

2   From the **TOC,Index** dialogue box choose **TOC OPTIONS...**

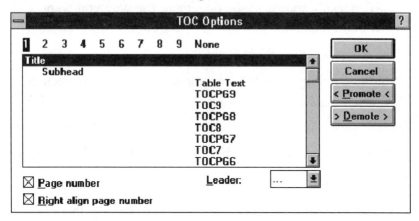

3   Promote or Demote the styles you're using to the TOC level required (you cannot have numerous paragraph styles at the same TOC level).

4   Select the checkboxes for **Page number** and **Right alignment** of page numbers if required. If you're using page numbers you can select a **Leader** character to run between the TOC entry and the page number.

5   Choose **OK** to return to the **TOC, Index** dialogue box and then **Cancel** to return to your document.

Apply the desired paragraph styles to the text you want to become TOC entries.

SPECIFYING SELECTED TEXT AS A TOC ENTRY

You can use this method instead of, or as well as, the method above - you can use both techniques to mark TOC entries in the same document if required.

You might want to use this method if your want a TOC entry and the text doesn't appear in the document the way you want it to appear in the TOC

OR

If you've got long headings, and you only want part of them as a TOC entry

OR

If you're not using heading paragraph styles to format the headings.

To do this you:-

1   Select the text you want to become a TOC entry or position the insertion point where you want to create your TOC entry

2   Choose **Edit, Mark Text, TOC Entry...**

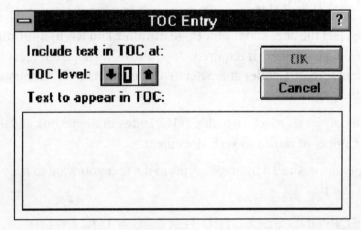

3   Edit or type the text that you want as your TOC entry if necessary

4   Assign the TOC level

5   Click **OK**

TO GENERATE A TABLE OF CONTENTS

Your Table of Contents can be generated to another file or at the beginning of your document. If you don't generate the TOC to another file, it appears as the first page in your document.

If your document has a Title Page or pages that must precede the TOC, you should generate the TOC to another document.

You must be in Layout Mode to generate your TOC.

1 Choose **Tools, TOC Index...**

2 Select the **Table of Contents** checkbox

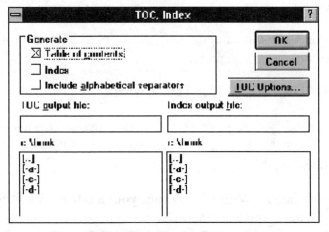

3 If you're generating your TOC to a different file, specify the drive, directory and filename for your TOC file.

4 If you didn't specify TOC levels for header paragraph styles, or page numbering requirements, choose **Options** and set up the options required. Choose **OK** to return to the **TOC, Index** dialogue box.

5 At the **TOC, Index** dialogue box choose **OK**.

The TOC is generated.

If you didn't specify an output file for the TOC, the insertion point is at the top of page 1 in the current document, at the beginning of the TOC (which will have been put before any other pages in your file). Ami Pro automatically creates and assigns paragraph styles to each entry. The styles are named TOC1-TOC9 and TOCPG1-TOCPG9.

If you specified a filename for your TOC, the insertion point is at the beginning of that file. The document uses the _TOC.STY style sheet and the paragraph styles from it.

The TOC is a Page Table and can be edited and modified like any other Table.

If you don't like the paragraph styles in _TOC.STY you can edit these to something you prefer.

MODIFY OR REMOVE A TOC ENTRY

You can modify or remove TOC entries generated from selected text. If you do this AFTER generating a TOC, you should regenerate the table to reflect the changes.

TOC entries are POWER FIELDS and you can choose **View, Show Power Fields** if you want them displayed in your document. You can then use **Edit, Powerfields, Next Field/Prev Field** to locate TOC Entries.

■ A *power field* is a tool you can use to automate document production. We won't be looking at power fields as a feature in its own right in this book, but you'll be introduced to a few as we go. Bookmarks, TOC entries and Index entries are only the beginning! Power fields are an advanced function you might want to investigate in the future.

Creating an Index is similar in concept to creating a TOC. There are 2 stages - telling Ami Pro WHAT is to appear in the Index, and actually generating the index itself.

You have a choice of 2 ways of telling Ami Pro WHAT to index. If you are creating an index for a document contained in one file, it's probably easiest to specify the index entries within that file. However, if you're creating an index for a large document, or you want to use the same index entries for several files, you'll find it easier to create a separate list document of index entries and use this for each file.

Let's look at the first method.

CREATING AN INDEX WITHIN A FILE

1 Within the document you want to create an index for, select the text for the index entry, or place the insertion point where the index entry will be

2 Choose **Edit, Mark Text, Index Entry...**

3 The **Mark Index Entry** dialogue box appears

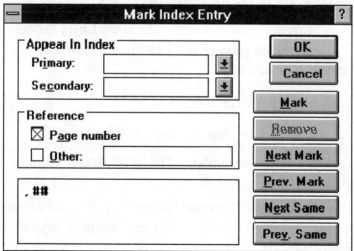

4   If you selected text, it appears in the **Primary** index field. If you didn't select text the insertion point appears in the **Primary** index field. If necessary edit or key in the entry.

5   If you've got index entries already you can view them by dropping down the list.

6   If you want the entry to be a **Secondary** Index Entry you must use the keyboard shortcuts to cut and paste it from the **Primary** field to the **Secondary** one (**Shift-Del** or **Ctrl-X** to Cut and **Shift-Ins** or **Ctrl-V** to Paste).

■   Make sure you choose the Primary Index entry you want your Secondary Index entry attached to *before* pasting the secondary index entry into the **Secondary** Index entry field.

7   Specify any **Reference** options desired. Choosing **Page number** places the number next to the entry when the index is generated.

8   You can use **Other** to specify any punctuation you want between the page number and any additional text you need to insert, ie *See* or *See Also* cross-references

9   Click **Mark** to create your entry. The **Mark Entry** dialogue box remains open so you acn mark additional entries for the sam paragraph if required.

TO GENERATE YOUR INDEX

You must be in Layout Mode to generate your Index.

1   Choose **Tools, Toc, Index...** The **TOC, Index** dialogue box appears

2   Select **Index** in the **Generate** options. If you want each section headed up alphabetically, select the **Include alphabetical separators** box.

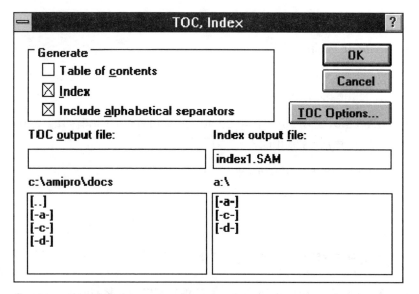

3 Specify the drive, directory and filename for your index (your index must go to an output file) and click **OK**.

4 If you haven't already saved your document file you will be prompted to do so. If it has already been saved Ami Pro will automatically save any changes to it.

The index is generated and your insertion point is placed at the beginning of your Index file.

The INDEX file uses the _INDEX.STY style sheet for its page layout and paragraph styles. You can modify the styles if you wish.

CREATING AN INDEX FROM AN INDEX LIST FILE

Use this method for indexing several similar files, or for indexing a large file that has many index entries referenced in multiple places within the file. Once your index list file is set up, you use it in each file you want to index - you don't need to type in the index entries again, you just mark the paragraphs you want indexed.

There are 5 stages to this:-

1   Type up the index list file

2   Mark the entries as primary or secondary level entries. Save and
    close the list file.

3   Insert the list file into your document and specify the paragraphs
    each entry has to index

4   Delete the list file from your document

5   Generate your index

Here goes!

TYPE UP THE INDEX LIST FILE

1   Open a New File using the _INDEX.STY style sheet.

2   Type up the list of PRIMARY entries exactly as you want them
    to appear in the final index - each entry should be a word or
    phrase on a line of its own (so press **Enter** at the end of each entry).

3   Apply the PRIMARY paragraph style to each of these entries.

4   SORT this list into alphabetical order

5   Type in any SECONDARY entries under the appropriate primary
    entries. Apply the SECONDARY paragraph style to these.

Once you've all the entries in, you're ready to mark them.

MARK THE ENTRIES AS PRIMARY OR SECONDARY
LEVEL ENTRIES

1   Go back to the beginning of your file (**Ctrl-Home**)

2   Select the first entry

3   Choose **Edit, Mark Text, Index Entry**

4 Complete the dialogue box as required and click **OK**

Do this for each entry - take care with the secondary level ones and be sure you put them under the appropriate primary level entry!

5 Save and close your Index List file.

INSERT THE INDEX LIST FILE AND MARK INDEX ENTRIES

1 Open the document that you are going to generate an Index for

2 Go to the end of the document (**Ctrl-End**) and put in a page break.

3 Choose **File, Open**

4 Select your **Index List** file and choose **Insert**

Your index list file is inserted at the end of your document.

5 Go back to the beginning of your document.

6 Put the insertion point in the first paragraph you want to create an index entry for

7 Choose **Edit, Mark Text, Index Entry...**

8 Select the first Primary or Secondary index entry you want to use and click **Mark**

9 Continue to do this until you've specified all the index entries required for that paragraph

10 Click **OK**

Do this for every paragraph you want an index entry for.

DELETE THE INDEX LIST FILE FROM THE DOCUMENT

Once you've marked all your index entries you must delete the Index List file from your document

1 Go to the beginning of the index list file

2 Select from there to the end of the document (**Shift-Ctrl-End**)

3 Press **Delete**

(If you don't delete your Index List file, the page numbers and entries on the Index you are about to generate will be inaccurate).

GENERATE YOUR INDEX

See above.

DON'T give your index the same name as your Index List File or you might overwrite it!! You want to keep your Index List File so you can use it again in another file.

EDITING YOUR INDEX

You can edit your index, by modifying an entry, adding new entries or removing existing entries.

Open the document from which the index is generated.

TO LOCATE AN INDEX ENTRY FOR EDITING

1 Choose **Edit, Mark Text, Index Entry...**

2 Flick back and forwards through the index entries using the **Next Mark, Prev Mark, Next Same** and **Prev Same** buttons, until you display the entry required.

MODIFY THE ENTRY

Once you've found the entry that you want to edit, make the desired changes and choose **Mark**.

ADD ANOTHER INDEX ENTRY

To add an index entry to a paragraph that already has one or more entries, display an existing index entry from the paragraph, key in the desired index entry for the new entry and choose **Mark**.

TO DELETE AN INDEX ENTRY

Display the index entry that is no longer required and choose **Remove**.

If you modify, add or remove index entries from your document after you've generated the index, you must regenerate the index to update it in line with your entries.

Index entries are POWER FIELDS and you can choose **View, Show Power Fields** if you want them displayed in your document. You can then use **Edit, Powerfields, Next Field/Prev Field** to locate index entries.

If you work with long documents - reports, manuals or books -and need to generate a table of contents or an index, you'll find this feature very useful.

Very often your long documents consist of a number of files - one for each section in a hefty report, or one for each section or chapter in a manual or book. When the document is complete, you need to generate a TOC or Index for the whole document -which is made up from several files. Enter the MASTER DOCUMENT feature!!

Using Ami Pro you can incorporate your files into a Master Document (which identifies the files that make up the final document) and you can generate a TOC or Index through it for your complete document. Wonderful!

The Master Document is assembled once you've created all the files that you're using.

Within each individual file, you should create your TOC and Index entries, assign paragraph styles and specify Index and TOC options. For best results (ie a consistent look to your final document) use the same heading paragraph styles in all files. It's also easier if you create an Index File List to makr your Index entries from.

TO CREATE THE MASTER DOCUMENT

You need to use a SOURCE document as your Master Document. This is simply the file you wish to be the Master Document file. You can open a new file for this, or you can use an existing document.

1 With the insertion point in the Master Document source file, choose **File, Master Document...**

The **Master Document** dialogue box appears.

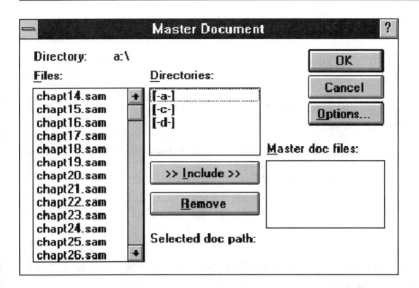

2 Specify the drive and directory that contains the files required

3 Select the first file you want in the Master Document and click **Include**

4 Select each file required in turn and Include it in the Master Document.

■ Include each file in the correct order, eg chapter1, chapter2, chapter3, to ensure the page numbering, TOC and Index are accurate!!!

5 Once you've included all your files, in the correct order, click **OK**.

■ If you accidentally add a file to your Master Document, you can select the file from the Master doc files: list and take it out by clicking **Remove**.

TO PRINT YOUR MASTER DOCUMENT

You can print your Master Document even if you haven't set up a TOC or Index

The insertion point must be in the Master Document (ie it's the Active Document)

Choose **File, Print ...** and complete the dialogue box as required

Ami Pro will print out the files specified in the Master Document keeping Page Numbering, Footnote Numbering and Outline Numbering Schemes consecutive over the files that make up the final document.

TO SET UP YOUR TOC OR INDEX FROM THE MASTER DOCUMENT

You can't generate a TOC or Index from a Master Document unless you've first marked all the entries required in the individual files (the previous 2 chapters tell you how to do this).

The insertion point must be in the Master Document file.

1   Choose **File, Master Document....**

2   At the **Master Document** dialogue box choose **Options**

    The **Master Document Options** dialogue box appears.

TABLE OF CONTENTS

1   If you want to generate a TOC for your master document, select the **Generate TOC** checkbox, and specify the drive, directory and filename for your output TOC file.

2   If you've used heading paragraph styles you can use the **TOC Options** to indicate the level of each paragraph style used.

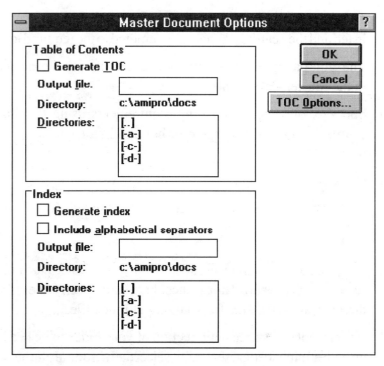

3 Choose **TOC Options** from the **Master Document Options** dialogue box

The **TOC Options** dialogue box appears

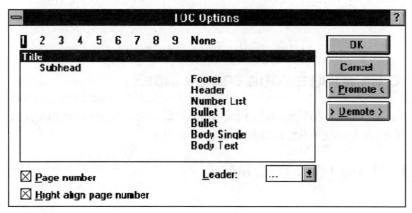

4 The paragraph styles available in your Master Document are listed and they can be promoted or demoted to the required level.

■ The same paragraph styles must be available in each file included in the Master Document!

5 Specify your page numbering requirements using the **Page number, Right align page number** and **Leader** boxes, at the bottom.

6 Click **OK** when done.

You return to the **Master Document Options** dialogue box.

INDEX

1 If you want to generate an Index from your Master Document select the **Generate Index** checkbox, and specify the drive, directory and filename for your output Index file.

2 If you want each alphabetic section of your Index to be headed up with an alphabetical separator, select the **Include alphabetical separator** box.

3 When you've completed specifying your requirements for the TOC or Index click **OK**.

You return to the **Master Document** dialogue box.

4 Click **OK** to return to the Source document.

TO GENERATE YOUR TOC OR INDEX

The insertion MUST be in the source document to generate your TOC or Index from a Master Document

1 Choose **Tools, TOC, Index...**

210

The options you set up in the **Master Document Options** dialogue box are displayed

2 Click **OK**

The TOC and Index are generated to their respective files.

TO MODIFY A MASTER DOCUMENT

The insertion point should be in the Master Document you want to modify

■ Choose **File, Master Document ...**

TO INCLUDE A FILE

1 Specify the drive and directory the required file is in

2 Select the file you want to include from the file list

3 Select the file that will go UNDER the one you are about to Include in the **Master Document Files** list

4 Click **Include**

■ (If you don't select a file in the Master Document files list, the new file is added to the end of the list)

TO REMOVE A FILE

1 Select the file you want to remove from the **Master Document Files** list

2 Click **Remove**

-7-
And Finally...

"System Management", "Housekeeping", "File Management" or whatever you want to call it is essential if you are to keep your disks and directories in order and your data safe.

If you save your data onto diskette (rather than onto the hard disk) you need to be able to format your diskettes. This can be done from Windows using **File Manager** - if you need to do this and don't know how, have a look at your Windows documentation under File Manager. The option is in the **Disk** menu.

Regardless of where you save your data (hard disk or diskette) you'll want to organise the storage space available to you. You can do this be creating Directories and Sub-directories. If you don't know how to do this, look at your Windows documentation under File Manager. The option is in the **File** menu.

From Ami Pro itself, you can manage your FILES - delete, copy, move, rename or view the files attributes (whether it's read-write or read only).

TO ACCESS FILE MANAGEMENT

1 Choose **File, File Management...**

The **File Manager** dialogue box appears.

```
┌─────────────────────────────────────────────────────────────────┐
│ ▬              Ami Pro File Manager                        ▼ ▲    │
├─────────────────────────────────────────────────────────────────┤
│ File  View  Help                                                 │
│                                                                  │
│  Directory:  c:\amipro\docs                                      │
│                                                                  │
│  File/Directory:        Description:                             │
│  ┌────────────────────────────────────────────────────────────┐ │
│  │ GOODIES.SAM     Ami Pro 3.0 macro descriptions.            │ │
│  │ MERCDATA.SAM    Famous sport figure database for Mail Merge│ │
│  │ MERCLET1.SAM    Letter anouncing Ami Pro                    │ │
│  │ MERCLET2.SAM    Letter to employees about AP               │ │
│  │ MERCURY.SAM     Main Mercury Demo file. Offers descriptions to many of the features in Ami Pro.│ │
│  │ README.SAM      This document contains important information about Ami Pro Reease 2.0.│ │
│  │ README30.SAM    README file for Ami Pro Release 3.0         │ │
│  │ TUTLTR.SAM      This is the working letter fle for the tutorial.│ │
│  │ [..]                                                        │ │
│  │ [-a-]                                                       │ │
│  │ [-c-]                                                       │ │
│  │ [-d-]                                                       │ │
│  └────────────────────────────────────────────────────────────┘ │
└─────────────────────────────────────────────────────────────────┘
```

2 Select the drive and directory required. To do this either double click the drive or directory required from the list or choose **File, Change Directory**

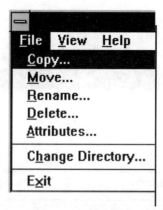

and specify the desired drive and directory in the dialogue box.

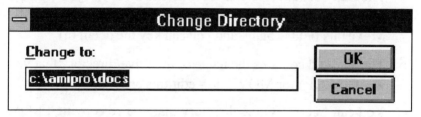

TO COPY OR MOVE A FILE

When you COPY a file, the original remains where it is and a copy of the file is put at the location indicated in the **To** field. You copy using the **File, Copy...** option in File Management.

If you find you've got a file in the wrong directory or on the wrong drive you can MOVE it using the **File, Move...** option in File Management. The file is removed from its original location and moved to the new one.

215

1   Select the file you want to copy or move from the file list (You can select multiple files by simply clicking on all the ones you want)

2   Choose **File, Copy....** or **File, Move ...**

3   The **Copy** or **Move File** dialogue box appears.

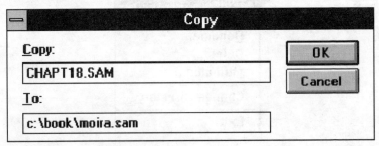

4   The **Copy** or **Move** field has the name of the file(s) you selected (if you didn't select a file before choosing **File, Copy** or **File, Move** this field is blank and you can key the detail in)

5   The **To** field contains the name or the drive/directory that you want to COPY or MOVE to - edit this as required.

■   You can't copy TO the directory that you're copying FROM unless you specify a different name for your file.

■   If you're copying or moving multiple files, or if you're copying a file but using the same filename, you just need to specify the drive and directory that you're copying the file(s) to.

6   Click **OK**

The **File Copy** or **File MoveOptions** dialogue box appears.

The Options let you specify whether the style sheet the document is based on and/or associated graphics files are copied with the document.

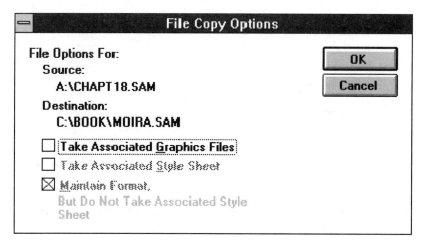

Using File Management to copy or move files is a reliable way of ensuring that your files are as you expect when you copy or move them - you can indicate exactly what you want to copy or move to maintain the contents of your document.

■   Using Windows or DOS doesn't guarantee that associated files are copied or moved when the main file is. Use Ami Pro when copying or moving your files - it's safer!!

7   Select the boxes required to indicate what should be copied or moved along with the main file and click **OK**.

TO RENAME A FILE

You can change the name of an existing file using the **File, Rename...** option in File Management.

1   Select the file you want to rename

2   Choose **File, Rename...**

3   The **Rename** dialogue box appears.

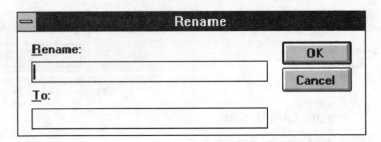

The name of the selected file appears in the **Rename** field (if you didn't select a filename, you can key the detail in)

4 Type in the name you want the file Renamed to in the **To** field and click **OK**.

The file remains on the drive and directory it was in, but has the name specified in the **To** field.

DELETE A FILE

1 Select the filename you want to delete

2 Choose **File, Delete...** (or press the **Delete** key on your keyboard)

The **Delete** dialogue box appears

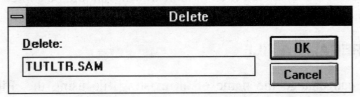

The name of the file selected appears in the dialogue box (if you didn't select one you can key in the detail).

3 Click **OK** to confirm the deletion.

ATTRIBUTES

You can check to see if a file is read-write or read-only using the **File, Attributes...** option.

1 Select the file you want to check the attributes of

2 Choose **File, Attributes.....**

The **File Attributes** dialogue box appears.

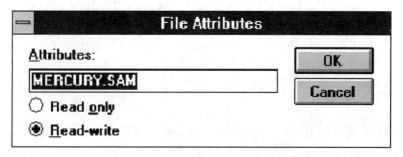

The name of the file you are checking is in the filename field.

The radio buttons indicate the read-write status of the file. **Read-write** files can be edited. Setting files to **Read only** protects finished documents from being accidentally changed.

3 If the read-write status is as you want it, you can leave the dialogue box by either clicking **OK** or **Cancel**.

4 If you want to change the read-write status, click the desired option, then leave the dialogue box by clicking **OK**.

VIEW OPTIONS

You can use the **View** menu in File Management to specify which files you want listed from the specified directory .

The options are:-

■ ***.S?M** files where all files with a **.S?M** extension (the **?** can be any character so you'll get **.SAM** and **.SMM** files)

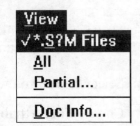

■ **ALL** gives you all files in the directory specified regardless of extension.

■ **Partial...** gives you a dialogue box to complete so you can indicate the file type required. Complete the dialogue box by typing ***** (an asterisk to indicate all filenames). (a dot to separate the filename from the extension) and the extension to select the file type you want. eg ***.TIF *.PCX**

DOC INFO

There may be times you want more information about a file before you copy, delete, move or rename it.

You can view this information using **View, Doc Info...**

1 Select the file you want information on

2 Choose **View, Doc Info...**

Any information recorded in Doc Info is displayed (you can't edit the information from here, you're just looking!).

TO EXIT FILE MANAGEMENT

1 Double click the control box or choose **File, Exit**.

When you name your files, the filenames can be up to a maximum of 8 characters long with an extension of 3 characters. No punctuation or spaces are permitted.

This can lead to some pretty cryptic filenames at times, and you might like to record additional information that helps you identify your files.

The additional information can be printed as a cover sheet for your file by choosing **File, Print, Options...** and checking the **With Document Description** box.

To record additional information about your active (current) file, choose **File, Doc Info...** The **Doc Info** dialogue box appears.

	Doc Info	?
File name: DOCINFO.SAM		**UK**
Directory: A:\		**Cancel**
Style sheet: None		**Other Fields...**

Description:

Keywords:

☐ **Lock for annotations**
☐ **Lock revision marking on**
☒ **Run frame macros**

Import files:

Date created:	10/5/93
Time created:	21:31

Statistics

No. of pages:	1	Size (K):	0
No. of words:	0		
No. of chars:	0	**Update**	

Date last revised:	10/5/93
Time last revised:	22:06
Total revisions:	2
Total editing time:	35

The file name, the directory it's saved in and the style sheet it's based on (none if you've opted to save the format with the document) are completed automatically.

You can give your file a Description (up to 119 characters) - this will appear in the dialogue box when you select the file in **File, Open** or **File, File Management**.

You can also insert some **Keywords** that will help describe the contents of the document to you.

Import Files gives the names of any source files that your file depends on for picture files or DDE links.

If you want other users to be able to add notes to your file but not edit it select the **Lock for Annotations** box.

If you want other users to edit your file, but you want to keep track of any insertions or deletions they make, select the **Lock Revision Marking On** box.

If you want Ami Pro to run any macros assigned to Frames select the **Run Frame Macros** box.

The other information in the dialogue box gives file statistics and date and time details on creation and editing.

You can add other information to your file by choosing **Other Fields...** You might want to record the author, department, recipient, operator. There are up to 8 other fields available. You can choose **Rename Fields...** and give the fields names that suit your needs and click OK.

The **Doc Info Fields** dialogue box.

MAIL

If you have either **cc:Mail for Windows** Release 1.1 or higher, or **Lotus Notes** Release 2.1 or higher, installed on your computer, you can send and receive messages from within Ami Pro.

TO SEND A MESSAGE

1 Open the document you want to attach to a message and make it the Active window (if you only want to send part of the document, select the text you want to send)

2 Choose **File, Send Mail**

3 Select **Attach** (If you selected text the Attach option is dimmed. If you edited the document since you last saved it, the Attach option reads **Save and Attach**.)

4 Choose **OK**

The Send Mail screen from the Mail application is displayed. Type in the mail message.

TO RECEIVE NOTIFICATION OF MAIL

If the Mail application is loaded, Ami Pro can notify you when you receive mail. Ami Pro checks with the Mail application every 5 minutes. If you've received anything, a **Mail** button displays on the status bar (an envelope). You can check your mail by clicking this button. Ami Pro displays the Mail application's Receive mail screen.

OTHER APPLICATIONS

At some stage you may find that you need to integrate Ami Pro with other applications you have. You may have data in a spreadsheet which you want to put into a company report or you might need to incorporate details from a database into your Ami Pro document, or you might need information from your Ami Pro document in another Windows application etc.

Full instructions on the various links possible can be found in the User's Guide but let's look at a couple of examples just to see how things work and to introduce you to some of the terminology.

You come across some new terminology when you get into linking and integrating applications so you're as well to get familiar with some of the terms. It's all standard Windows stuff!

In Windows you use either **DDE** (Dynamic Data Exchange) or **OLE** (Object Linking and Embedding) to share information between applications. Not ALL Windows applications support DDE and OLE.

Using either of these utilities, you can create a **LINK** between files in different Windows applications.

With every LINK there is a **SERVER** (the application that holds the original data and provides it to other applications) and a **CLIENT** (the application that uses the data provided by the Server).

With **DDE links**, both applications must be running simultaneously if amendments made in the Server file are to be accurately reflected in the Client file (this obviously takes up a lot of memory).

With an **OLE link**, the object becomes embedded in the Client file, and the Server application is closed. It is however a simple matter to open the server application and edit the embedded object as required.

Let's have a look at an example of each.

225

DYNAMIC DATA EXCHANGE (DDE)

A fairly typical requirement may be the inclusion of spreadsheet data (probably from 1-2-3 for Windows) into a report in Ami Pro. You might also require the data in the Ami Pro document (the Client) to be updated whenever the data in the 1-2-3 spreadsheet (the Server) is updated.

The procedure for this is quite straightforward.

1   Open the spreadsheet that contains the data you want in 1-2-3 for Windows

2   Select the range of cells required and choose **Edit, Copy**

3   Leave 1-2-3 running (you can minimise its window to clear the desktop a bit)

4   Go into Ami Pro and open the document you need the data in

5   Place the insertion point where you want to paste the spreadsheet data (if you want it in a table, create a table of the correct size first and place the insertion point in the first cell to paste into)

6   Use **Edit, Paste Link** to place the spreadsheet data into Ami Pro

Any changes made to data in 1-2-3 will automatically update the data in the Ami Pro report as long as the link is active - this requires both applications to be running.

OBJECT LINKING AND EMBEDDING

OLE enables you to create a single document in Windows using several Windows applications. The original data becomes an OBJECT in the document in which it is embedded. If you need to edit the object, you simple double click on it and you are taken into the Server application to edit it.

The procedure is as below:-

1 Open the Ami Pro document into which you want to embed the object

2 Create, size and select an empty frame - or you can let Ami Pro do this automatically using the default frame settings when you insert the object

3 Choose **Edit, Insert, New Object**.

The **Insert New Object** dialog box appears, listing all applications you have, that support OLE and the types of objects they create.

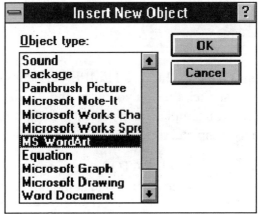

4 Select the **Object type** required (the example below was done using MS WordArt) and click **OK**.

5 Create the object you require.

6 Choose **File, Update** (not necessary in MS WordArt) to save the object and, if necessary, **File, Exit** to exit the application and return to your Ami Pro document.

To edit the embedded object, simply double click the object to start the Server application and edit the object as required.

Creating complex looking equations is easy with Ami Pro. If you have exam papers to prepare or equations to insert into a document, you'll find this feature very useful.

To create an equation, choose **Tools, Equations...**

Ami Pro creates a FRAME for your equation (the default has no lines or borders but you can modify it as required), the Equation icons appear and an **Equation** menu appears on the Menu bar.

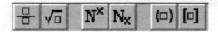

The first 6 icons on the top line are TEMPLATE icons - to choose a template you just click the one you want and it's inserted at the insertion point. Each template icon consists of symbols and input boxes for you to complete.

The next 2 are OPERATOR icons - again just point and click to insert the desired one at the insertion point.

The next 2 are TOGGLE icons. The **M** indicates that Ami Pro thinks everything you're inserting is a mathematical symbol or operator - if you want to key some text symbols into your equation click the button to toggle over to **T** for text, then Ami Pro knows you're inserting text characters and not mathematical ones. The * toggles between show/hide input boxes and matrix lines (these lines don't print out but you might find it easiest to show them so you can see exactly where you are in your equation).

The last 8 in the top row (the ones with ... under them) are DIALOGUE BOX icons. You can use these to specify exactly what symbol, template, characters or functions you want to enter.

On the bottom row you have SYMBOL icons - you can insert any of the symbols at the insertion point by clicking the one you want.

The PULLDOWN BOX icons give you access to many more symbols in addition to those displayed on the symbol icons.

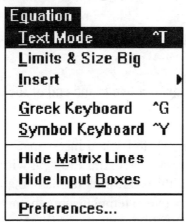

You can use the **Equation** menu to give commands if you prefer - have a browse and see what there is in the icon dialogue boxes, pulldown box icons and the equation menu option!

All the symbols and functions you want are available through the icons. The easiest way to get the hang of this is to try it out.

Let's say you wanted to produce $x = \sqrt{\dfrac{3}{17} - b^2 - k}$

1 Position the insertion point where you want to key in the equation and choose **Tools, Equations...**

2 Type **x=**

3 Click the **square-root** icon template (2nd one in top row), then the **fraction** icon template (1st one on top row).

4 Type the **3** in the top input box, press **Tab**, type **17** in the lower input box.

(You can use the mouse, the tab key or the cursor keys to move from input box to input box).

5 Press the **Spacebar** to move to the end of the expression.
Type **-b**

6 Click the **superscript** template icon (3rd one on top row).
Type **2**

7 Press the **Spacebar** to move to the end of the expression

Type **-k**

DON'T use the spacebar to try and insert spaces to separate the elements of your equation - let Ami Pro deal with this for you to begin with. Spacing that conforms to mathematical typesetting conventions is used between templates, mathematical characters, symbols and functions. If you need to customise a space use the **Space** dialogue box icon (4th from right, top row).

DO experiment placing the insertion point in the input boxes using the mouse, tab and cursor keys - sometimes it's tricky getting the right place until you get used to it. It's just a case of recognising when the insertion point is actually IN an input box and when it's not.

Let's try something a bit trickier! Use the spacebar or the mouse to move the insertion point to the end of the expression when necessary.

$$\int_c^d f(x)bx = \lim \frac{d-c}{n} \sum_{r=1}^{n} \left(c + \frac{r}{n}(d-c) \right)$$

1 From the **Operator** dialogue box (the 1st dialogue box icon on top row), choose the **single integral** operator, and select **At Right** and **Auto**.

2 Click the **Superscript** template icon

Type in **d**, press **TAB**, and type in **c**

3 Move to the end of the expression

Type in **f**

4 Click the **Parentheses** icon template (5th one in)
Type in **x**

5 Move to the end of the expression

Type in **bx=**

6 From the **Function** dialogue box (4th one) choose **lim**, select **Auto**, click **OK**

7 Choose the **Fraction** template icon

Type **d-c**, press **Tab**, type **n**

8 Move to the end of the expression

9 From the **Operator** dialogue box choose the **Summation** operator, select **Limit Position Above/Below** and click **OK**

10 Click the **Superscript** template icon

Type **n**, press **Tab**, type **r=1**

11 Move to the end of the expression

12 Click the **Parentheses** template icon

Type **c+**

13 Click the **Fraction** template icon

Type **r**, press **Tab**, type **n**

14 Move to the end of the expression

15 Click the **Parentheses** template icon again

Type **d-c**

16 Use the mouse or press the **Spacebar** twice to move to the end of the expression

Pretty neat!!

TO MOVE FROM YOUR EQUATION INTO YOUR DOCUMENT

Click anywhere outside the frame your equation is in.

TO EDIT AN EXISTING EQUATION

Double click anywhere inside the frame containing the equation. The equation icons and the Equation Menu option appear and you can edit your equation as necessary. You can select parts of your equation using click and drag or Click/Shift-click techniques then delete, copy or move as required.

TO DELETE AN EQUATION

Select the equation frame then press the **Delete** key.

Macros simply provide a way of recording routines that you do regularly, to allow you to playback, or re-run, them whenever you need to.

We've already looked at several ways of recording text that you need to use repetitively - in Glossaries or in Merge situations. We've also looked at Styles as a method of recording formatting information.

With Macros you can also record text or formatting instructions if you wish, but where they differ, is in that you can record routines as well. For example you can use a macro to record a special print routine and specification that you need for some of your documents, or to generate special characters at a keystroke.

I'm NOT going to attempt to cover macros in detail with you in this book - but to simply make you aware that they exist and whet your appetite for what they might offer you. Once you're confidently finding your way around the package, and feel the need to automate some of the more standard routines you have to perform, then that's when you want to investigate the Macro!

READY-MADE MACROS

You don't have to create your own macros to use them as Ami Pro comes with 40 useful macros ready for you to use. It's a good idea to have a look through them to see what might be of interest to you.

All the details are in a file called GOODIES.SAM which would have been installed when you installed Ami Pro. Have a read through it and see what's there.

Try out any that sound interesting.

TO PLAYBACK A MACRO

To playback a macro, one supplied with Ami Pro or one you've written yourself, choose **Tools, Macros, Playback** and select the macro file from the dialogue box.

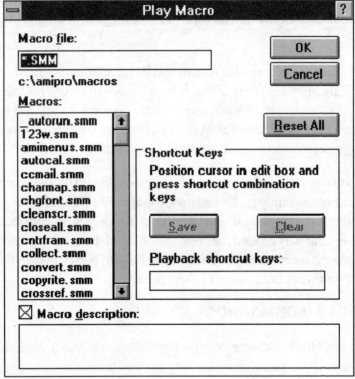

Try playing back these ones.

CHARMAP.SMM - if you run this macro a new option **Special Character...** is added to the **Edit, Insert** menu option. You can then access all sorts of things -

Life becomes such fun!!

To get the characters:

1 Choose **Edit, Insert, Special Character...**.

2 Browse through the character maps until you find something that you want, point and click to select it.

3 Click the **Select** button to copy the character to the **Copy Character** field.

4 Repeat this process until you've got the characters you want.

5 Click the **Copy** button to copy the selected characters to the Clipboard.

6 Close the character map window.

7 The characters you selected are copied into your document at the insertion point. You can then move them or resize them if necessary.

COPYRITE.SMM inserts the © symbol at the insertion point.

TM.SMM inserts the ™ symbol at the insertion point.

INDEXALL.SSM marks all occurrences of a word for indexing.

WORDCNT.SMM adds a new option **Word Count...** to the **View** menu.

You can record your own Macros to automate routines you perform regularly.

TO RECORD A MACRO

1 Choose **Tools, Macros, Record...**

2 Give your Macro file a name (Ami Pro will automatically give it a .SMM extension).

3 Perform the functions you want to record in the Macro (note the Recording Macro prompt on the Status Bar). EVERYTHING you key in will be recorded - mistakes as well!

4 When you're finished choose **Tools, Macros, End Record**.

QUICK RECORD AND QUICK PLAYBACK

You can also use the **Tools, Macros, Quick Record** and **Quick Playback** options.

This lets you set up a temporary macro (perhaps one that's going to be useful for the document you're working in, but not something you want to save as a macro file for future use).

The only difference between this and recording a macro into a special macro file is that the macro is placed in a file called UNTITLED.SMM. The macro is not saved to disk, and each time you create a new Quick Macro, the previous one is overwritten.

Use **Tools, Macros, Quick Playback** to playback your quick macro.

If you decide you want to save a macro recorded as a quick macro, open UNTITLED.SMM and use **File, Save As** to save it under a different file name.

EDITING A MACRO

If you are editing a short macro, it's probably easiest to overwrite the original one with the new version (just record the macro again, using the same filename and opt to overwrite the original when you're prompted).

If you need to edit a Macro that's quite long and complex, you can choose **Tools, Macros, Edit...** and select the macro file you want to edit.

1 Your macro file is opened into its own window.

A macro opened in this way is displayed in MACRO LANGUAGE - a macro recorded as

Yours sincerely

Moira Stephen

looks like this in **Macro, Edit...**

FUNCTION MOIRA1()
Type("Yours sincerely[Enter][Enter][Enter][Enter][Enter]
Moira Stephen")
Type("[Enter]")
END FUNCTION

2 Don't panic!!

3 When making the changes required, follow the layout you see - ie precede any keyboard characters with **Type("** and finish off with **")**. If you want a return - type **[Enter]** into your macro.

4 Save the edited version - Ami Pro compiles the macro when you choose **File, Save**.

5 Close your file.

We've only touched the tip of the iceberg with Macros. Don't be put off by the Macro Language - you can record and playback macros without using it! Keep things simple to begin with - try creating macros for repetitive print routines, or print merge routines or to insert any bullets that you like using.

Use the on-line help and the manual (they're really quite helpful once you know your way about).

If you're used to using Macros and/or programming you'll find a lot of information in **Help, Macro Doc...** to help you become quickly accustomed to the Macro Language.

Have fun!!

Index

Index

Index

Index

Index

I

K

L

M

O

Index

Index

Index

T

U

Index